Modern Poetry in Tr

Series Three, Number

The Dialect of the Tribe

Edited by David and Helen Constantine

MODERN POETRY IN TRANSLATION

Modern Poetry in Translation
Series Three, No. 16
© Modern Poetry in Translation 2011 and contributors
ISBN 978-0-9559064-8-0

Printed and bound in Great Britain by Charlesworth Press, Wakefield

Submissions should be sent in hard copy, with return postage, to David
and Helen Constantine, *Modern Poetry in Translation*, The Queen's College,
Oxford, OX1 4AW. Unless agreed in advance, submissions by email will
not be accepted. Only very exceptionally will we consider work that has
already been published elsewhere. Translators are themselves responsible
for obtaining any necessary permissions, and should be aware that work
published in *MPT* may also appear on our website and as an e-book, and
will be accessible to readers who have subscribed to the digital version of
the magazine.

Subscription Rates: (including postage)

	UK	Overseas
Single Issue	£9.95	£12.50 / US$ 21
One year subscription (2 issues, surface mail)	£19.90	£25.00 / US$ 42
Two year subscription (4 issues, surface mail)	£36.00	£46.00 / US$ 77

To subscribe please use the subscription form at the back of the magazine.
Discounts available.

To pay by credit card please visit www.mptmagazine.com

Modern Poetry in Translation is represented in the UK by
Central Books, 99 Wallis Road, London, E9 5LN

For orders: tel +44 (0) 845 458 9911 Fax +44 (0) 845 458 9912
or visit www.mptmagazine.com

Modern Poetry in Translation Limited. A Company Limited by Guarantee.
Registered in England and Wales, Number 5881603.
UK Registered Charity Number 1118223.

Contents

Editorial

The UN has 193 members – that is, it recognizes 193 states. Some of these member-states recognize other states which are not members, which means that even to the question, 'How many nation-states are there in the world?', the answer will vary according to who (and when) you ask. And there is far less agreement as to how many languages Earth speaks. One scholar's (or interested party's) language is another's mere dialect or idiom. The 1911 *Encyclopaedia Britannica,* put the figure at around 1000. The current estimate is around 7000.

However else a nation-state may be defined, it may *not* be defined as a geographical unit of language. Languages are no more contained within the shape and frontiers of a nation than are wild flowers, seeds, rivers, fish, butterflies, clouds or migrating birds.

Carl Linnaeus in the mid-18th century named 10,000 species of life on earth. The latest estimate is 8.7 million. Continually we discover more, and idly or quite deliberately endanger and exterminate more and more among those we name and know. Twenty years ago Edward O. Wilson estimated that 27,000 species go into – are dispatched into – extinction every year. 'I had not thought death had undone so many . . .'

Languages are dying too. One a fortnight. Perhaps half of our 7000 will be gone by 2100. Such a peculiar hallmark ours, this drive and drift into mass extinction. In the Permian, long before we were here, 95% of life on earth vanished. But that was thanks to an asteroid, it wasn't engineered by the most intelligent creatures then present.

A people's self-identity springs in large measure from its language. For that reason when one people or nation annexes another, or wishes to homogenize itself, it will control or even seek to exterminate the languages within its frontiers by which heterogeneity is signalled and asserted. So Franco acted against Basque and Catalan; in some Welsh schools in the 19th century any child heard speaking Welsh was made to wear a little collar, a wooden tablet, on which was written WN, that is: 'Welsh Not'; the French, when they got Alsace back in 1919, forbade the speaking of German; the Germans, returning in the summer of 1940, forbade the speaking of French (speakers of Alsatian were given five years to learn German and in the meantime were isssued with a permit to speak their 'dialect' among themselves). And so on. Any number of instances. Stop their language, stop their voice. Without a voice, they are at your mercy. Tony Harrison said it in his poem 'National Trust':

> The dumb go down in history and disappear
> And not one gentleman's been brought to book:
> *Mes den hep tavas a—gollas y dyr*
> (Cornish) –
> > 'the tongueless man gets his land took.'

These things are very well known. After such knowledge, what is to be done? Well at least we can try to stop it happening now.

T.S. Eliot's 'Little Gidding', from which we took the phrase that is the title of this issue, was completed in September 1942 and first published the following month in *The New English Weekly*. Ned Thomas (see p. 24) comments wryly on 'the familiar compound ghost' who speaks the words. Here is their immediate context: 'Since our concern was speech, and speech impelled us/ To purify the dialect of the tribe . . .' Surely even then that line must have had a sinister tone? Nowadays, after the opening of the camps and the archives, and with yet more added and still being added to the list of cleansings, it sends a shudder through the soul. Between the first draft of 'Little Gidding', August 1941, and its completion, Reinhard Heydrich, directed by Goering, prepared the measures for the Final Solution of the Jewish Question and presented them to the responsible officers at the Wannsee Conference on 20 January 1942, after which they were implemented. No one in England could have known about Wannsee, but most did know by then, or should have known, about the Nuremberg Laws, *Kristallnacht* and the mass emigration and exiling of Jews and many others the Reich wanted rid of.

Doubtless Eliot's ghost had his own dialect in mind, the language that, as a poet, he felt responsible for and needed to 'purify' – the better, as the next line puts it, 'to urge the mind to aftersight and foresight. Still, 'purify' is wrong.

Many nations have at one time or another sought to purify the national language. German during the Thirty Years War was grievously adulterated by the Spanish, French, Italian, English, Croat, Swedish and heaven knows what else criss-crossing its territory with the armies. Academies were founded and individual writers engaged themselves to protect the native speech. *Fremdwörter* (as they are called) stand out in German more than they do in English, and are thus more offensive to purists. In the Third Reich a new linguistic purism ran with the racial. Nowadays the French are notably anxious about words riding in from across the Channel and the Atlantic.

Even within the nation there may be one class or district which claims to speak the purest and only proper dialect and on that basis despises all speakers of anything else. Tuscans, Hanoverians, Castilians have all thought theirs was it. And how uncomfortable so many millions of English have been made to feel by the inventors and enforcers of Queen's English and RP. Ye are many, they are few! But how long it has taken for the many to disenthral themselves. Now not even the Queen speaks her English as purely as she used to (old recordings prove it) and there was something almost touchingly out-of-touch in David Starkey's contribution to our understanding of the recent riots. The chavs have become black, he said, the language of the streets is now Jamaican patois, so that he feels, poor chap, like a foreigner in his own country. (See the Language Log website for an explanation of what Jamaican patois actually is.)

Five hundred languages are spoken in London. And if you want to hear how beautifully various one of them, English, is, go to the British Library (or their website) and listen in to their thesaurus of speaking voices. 'Evolving English', they have called it: 'One language, many voices.'

And there we have it, in that nutshell. There were lexicographers in the 18th century who wished not just to record but also to *fix* the national language in their volumes, believing it to have reached its best and final form. As though you could legislate a language into fixity! A language must evolve or die, all its speakers may contribute to its life. And every speaking voice of a language is unique, every person's speech is an ideolect, every poet's language is as distinguishable as his or her DNA. Translating a poem, you mix your own voice with the poet's. Thus doubly flighted, poems pass over the frontiers like seeds.

David and Helen Constantine
August 2011

The Next Issue of *MPT*

The next issue of *Modern Poetry in Translation* (Third Series, Number 17, Spring 2012) will be called 'Parnassus'.

This issue will be largely given over to a collaboration with 'Poetry Parnassus' – the Southbank Centre's celebration of the 2012 London Olympics. Poets from all 205 participating countries will be invited to London and *MPT* will be a place where some translations of their poems can be published. But, to enlarge our contribution, we want translated poems, brief essays, anecdotes and images concerned, in whatever fashion, with the Games (ancient or modern) or with Parnassus, home of the Muses. Parnassus was a sacred site for the whole Greek world; Delphi, below that mountain, was 'the navel of the earth'; for the duration of the Olympics a truce was declared so that athletes could come and go safely. The modern Olympics are world–wide: we want *MPT* 3/17 to be just as extensive and various.

Submissions should be sent by 1 February 2012, please, in hard copy, with return postage, to The Editors, *Modern Poetry in Translation*, The Queen's College, Oxford, OX1 4AW. Unless agreed in advance, submissions by email will not be accepted. Only very exceptionally will we consider work that has already been published elsewhere. Translators are themselves responsible for obtaining any necessary permissions. Contributors should be aware that work published in *MPT* may also appear on our website and as an e-book, and will be accessible to readers who have subscribed to the digital version of the magazine.

MPT Poetry Translation Competition

Translate any poem on the subject of FREEDOM into English verse. The poem may be in any language, from any age, and in translation should not exceed twenty lines.

Entries (£4 per poem/£3 for subscribers) by 1 January 2012, may be sent via our website, www.mptmagazine. com on payment of the entry fee. Alternatively hard copy and cheque to Queen's College Oxford, OX1 4AW. Please include the original text with your translation.

Judges: David Constantine, Helen Constantine,
Sasha Dugdale.

First prize: £150

Second prize: £75

Three runners-up: one year's free subscription to *MPT*

All winners and runners-up will have their poems published in the Spring issue of *MPT*.

Entries should not have been published elsewhere. Translators are themselves responsible for obtaining any necessary permissions, and should be aware that work published in MPT may also appear on our website and as an e-book, and will be accessible to readers who have subscribed to the digital version of the magazine.

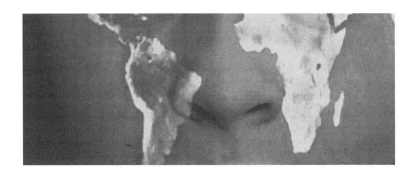

David Morley
Reforging the 'Broken Language'
Romani Poetry

The dialect of my tribe is Romani. *Sorì simensar sì mèn*: 'We are all one: all who are with us are ourselves.' I am Romani and I am *Gaji*.

Gaji is Romani for non-Romani.

Here is my story.

My mother is a *Poshrat*, a half-blood Rom. She is the seventh child of a seventh child and claims to possess second sight among other powers. During my childhood in the 1970s we were bitingly poor. My father had died young so my mother strove to earn a living by shape-changing overnight from pseudo-*Gaji* to Romani. What she did was valiant. My mother's Roma identity provided the means for some local distinction. Identity – not money – picked us up from the floor of grief and poverty. We traded in the silver of family history and mythology, caring little for the fault line between fact and fiction. It was an apprenticeship in blagging. I wrote and sold my first stories and articles at the age of twelve disguising my age with a cheap typewriter.

We lived in Blackpool. The tide of people moved in and out every week whether those days were bright or brown. Blackpool was a fairground. The town stretched its adolescent summer into October by illuminating the promenade with chains of light, rocket trams and electric tableaux. Then Blackpool withered into a ghost town until Easter. Blackpool liked Gypsies when they made money and paid taxes. Gypsies rented booths on Blackpool seafront and told fortunes. They displayed photographs of themselves with celebrities. Gypsies read Tarot cards, unveiled crystal balls, flogged white heather and rag-and-boned.

We did a fair bit of 'Gypsying' ourselves in the 1970s. Oddly enough, in a *Gaji* town like Blackpool there was still awareness of caste. *Gaji* were superior to the Roma. Roma were a head above the Gypsies. Gypsies pulled rank on Irish tinkers who themselves towered over tramps. I did not subscribe to a caste-check between Romani and *Gaji*. I knew some Roma had little time for *Gaji* while every *Gaji* looked down on Roma, even when they themselves dressed up as Gypsies and danced flamenco badly. As we might say, *Mendi shom sorkon cheerus kairin' a godli yek te waver* – to which I offer no translation.

My mother nurtured remarkable prejudices against so-called non-Roma travellers and tinkers. When they knocked on our door to sell pegs or lucky heather she sent them packing. They cursed us but she counter-blasted with a superior Roma Curse that never quite seemed to work. Nevertheless she believed in her powers with all her heart. To my horror (and to my family's delight) the one time I ever cursed a fellow man I killed him. I was sixteen. A local *Gaji* criminal called The Finn had been threatening our family for years, and was trying to fit me up with crimes he had committed. I called him out on the street and spat on his shoes, cursing him briefly but coldly. I was dizzy with rage and amazed to escape the encounter in one piece (I had not known the gangster was asthmatic). The Finn was arrested the next day and died in his police cell overnight. I was appalled. My folks were exultant. My mother saw it as 'the powers' passing forward. I saw it as the police withholding The Finn's inhaler:

Later, he was lights out on a cell floor.
The coppers let him ride out his asthma.
By the evening, he was old.
At dawn, they found him cold.
Runt Finn, they said, you're running nowhere.
Finn of the Wiles. Finn of the Filch, with his pickers and stealers.
I saw him out of depth a hare in the open,
antennal ears, rickety lope,
dodging the police on The Golden Mile.
In a swirl of litter, something or nothing the shape of him.

(from 'Finn of the Wiles')

This unshining example of my behaviour shows how some Gypsies allied themselves with spiritualistic pursuits. There was glamour to the terror of visiting *o kole doonyaste*, the other world. My mother said she could read your future in your hand (she even had library books on the subject). She held séances and read the Tarot for paying customers. Money talked in Blackpool and my mother could make the dead talk for a price:

Picture how a claw hammer angles under a settled nail,
grinds against the top grain, then slides out the clean metal
fresh from first hammering. Rosa works her audience,
and with her claw for grief, she plies her darkened séance.
An unknown sound is ground for a gnomic reading.
Ghosts arrive on time. Her daughter's upstairs frapping
the floor: one tap for 'no', twice for 'yes', with three
slow *bumps* for some spiritualistic ambiguity.

(from 'Smoke, Mirror')

There were famous Gypsies in Blackpool: the tribe that built The Pleasure Beach in the sand-hills of South Shore (the site of a traveller camp in the late 19th century) were millionaires. To be Gypsy, to be Roma, was acceptable if exotic. You would not want to boast about it for fear of a brick through the window (it

would have been a mistake to speak Romani). On the other hand
it helped you get by. As a family we were half-in and half-out
of mainstream culture but this liminal state appeared to be the
condition of travelling people. It was as absurd to talk about a
pure Romani as it is now for the BNP to sell the notion of an
indigenous Briton. Liminality and admixture are the conditions
of our people, and of our language Angloromani.

There is neither a pure Romani language nor a pure English
language. There are varieties of tongue and dialect and idiom in
any living, shifting form of speech and writing. There are several
Romani dialects: some are still with us, some are tattered, and
some are left behind. The Angloromani dialect is a mash-up of
loan words, Romani and English. How does Angloromani work
on the page or in speech? In his provocatively titled *Romani in
Britain: The Afterlife of a Language,* the linguist Yaron Matras
explains how Angloromani 'consists of embedding a special
lexical reservoir, largely derived from Romani, into English con-
versation . . . Contemporary Angloromani thus remains the living
speech variety of one of Britain's oldest and most established
ethnic minorities'. Angloromani is macaronic by necessity and
design; its poetry is usually macaronic in its diction and syntax.
Were I retuning the King James Version of 'The Song of Songs'
it would sound something like this:

> As the parnò looloodì among karòs, so is mi dèhiba among
> her cshays.
> Stay me with flagons, comfort me with aphai: for I am
> nasvalòo of kamav.
> For I charge you, o ye cshays of Jerusalem, by the surnà, and
> by the surnà of the oomalyàkom, that ye stir not up, nor
> awake mi dèhiba, till mangàva.
> Looloodì appear on the doonyàs, the tsìros of chiriklògìlyaiba
> is come, and the sèsi of the goorgoorìtsa is heard in our
> phoov.
> Take us to the weshjooks, the tsikooroo weshjooks, that spoil
> the vitsa: for amarò vitsa have parus drakhà.

Until sabàlen, and the oochipè flees away, ìrin, mi dèhiba, and be thou like a roe or a ternò surnà upon the plàyna of Bether.

I will rise now, and go about the fòros in the òolitsa, and in the boohlò putèka I will seek him, my ozì piryamlòo: I sought him, amà I found him not.

Avàv from Lebanon, my rom, avàv from Lebanon: dikhav from the hip of Amana, from the hip of Shenir and Hermon, from the dens of aslàni, from the plàyna of leopards.

Ko adavkhà that cometh out of the wilderness like pillars of thoov, smelling of myrrh and frankincense, with all powders of the Roma?

Spikenard and saffron; calamus and cinnamon, with all trees of frankincense; myrrh and aloes, with sòvra spices.

For King Solomon has made himself a vardo of the kash of Lebanon.

parnò looloodì: white flower (lily); **har:** valley; **karòs:** thorns, stings (n.); **cshays:** daughters; **aphai:** apples; **nasvalòo:** sick; **kamav:** love; **surnà:** deer; **oomalyàkom:** field; **mangàva:** wishes, pleases; **looloodì:** flowers; **doonyàs:** earth; **tsìros:** time; **chiriklògìlyaiba:** singing of birds; **sèsi:** voice; **goorgoorìtsa:** dove; **phoov:** land; **weshjooks:** foxes; **tsikooroo weshjooks:** little foxes; **vitsa:** vine; **amarò:** our; **parus:** soft; **drakhà:** grapes; **sabàlen:** daybreak; **oochipè:** shadow; **ìrin:** turn around; **ternò surnà:** young deer; **plàyna:** mountain; **fòros:** city; **òolitsa:** streets; **boohlò:** broad; **putèka:** paths; **ozì piryamlòo:** soul's lover; **amà:** but; **avàv:** come (imp.); **rom:** husband, spouse; **dikhav:** look; **hip:** top; **aslàni:** lions; **ko adavkhà:** who is this; **thoov:** smoke; **Roma:** gypsy (travelling merchant); **sòvra:** all; **vardo:** wagon; **kash:** wood.

Yet there is more to the Romani language's intention than playing two sides of a tongue. It is also a language that travels

forward with two minds simultaneously alert and calculating the
odds. Consider the expression *The tatcho drom to be a jinney-mengro
is to shoon, dick and rig in zi.* This could read as 'the true way to
be a wise man is to hear, see and bear in mind.' Buried in the
final clause is a *come-on* to do something utterly unpredictable,
to perform the very last thing you might expect a person (or
a poem) to do. Layered, nuanced, prismatic, Angloromani is a
survivor's tongue and has survived much breakage. I opened this
essay by quoting the expression *Sorì simensar sì mèn*: 'We are all
one: all who are with us are ourselves.' The first idea is benign
but the fist of the phrase is that if you are not with us you are an
outcast to the universe. It is a curse-in-waiting – an *akooshìba* – as
well as being a blessing in anticipation:

> Remember: we are all one: all who are with us are ourselves.
> Our word gallops like grass-fires. You will wither by this
>   word.
>
> I will crash through your kingdoms, calling your kanilipè
> to the realms of all Roma. I am riding revenge to you,
>
> to the lip and leap of a distant devlèskere pògya.
> O dooymooyalò, judge me, but you will remember me.
>
> Hold the halter of patsyàva. I am riding this curse on you.
> I wage war with these words, on your raklò and raklì.
>
> Remember I rank you, as shtòopos, as sapnì.
> You are ratvalyaràv, randimè. You rise only to be reaped.
>
> Your names now are nangò, your newborn cshoongadimè.
> Cshavàlen who chastised us, we who are chindi-chibengoro.
>
> You will remember me. You will meet me in your mirror,
> for I am the asking and answering owlcalls of an akooshìba.

kanilipè: evil-doing; **devlèskere pògya**: horizon;
dooymooyalò: hypocrite, double-dealer; **patsyàva**: belief;
raklò: non-Gypsy boy; **raklì**: non-Gypsy girl; **shtòopos**:
rubbish, garbage; **sapnì**: snake; **ratvalyaràv**: covered with
blood; **randimè**: reaped; **nangò**: naked ; **cshoongadimè**:

bespattered ; **Cshavàlen**: O You People!; **chindi-chibengoro**: without a tongue.

(from 'Kings')

In his study, Yaron Matras remarks:

> British Romanies are very much aware of a 'lost' form of language that was once used for a wide range of conversational functions within their community . . . It has even left a legacy within English in the form of Romani-origin colloquial words like *pal*, *chavvy*, *mush*, *minge* and *kushti* as well as regionalisms like *gaji*, *nash*, *peeve*, *ladj* and *yocks*. Its decline as the everyday language of the Romani community took place during the nineteenth century, when other languages of the British Isles were also being abandoned in favour of English. However, in a way Romani has actually survived the process of language death and now enjoys a kind of linguistic 'afterlife': Romanies in Britain continue to use a variety of speech which they refer to as *Rommanis*, *Romimus*, *Romani Jibb* 'the Romani language', or sometimes *Poggadi Jibb* 'the broken language'.

My experience as a writer is that Romani speech acts are as dead or broken as you make them, and that just because a language is declared *poggadi* or even lifeless does not mean it cannot be melted, reforged and hammered back into being. A language is not *like* a way of life, it *is* a way of life. It might die through occupation by other languages or because it has lost function. Yet a language can also die through a lack of imagination. Despite the obituary, the apparent afterlife of Angloromani provides a fertile environment for its reinvention. To my mind, and in my practice as a poet, Angloromani offers a potential for literary invention similar to that which Lallans offered to Hugh MacDiarmid in the early part of the twentieth century. Here is my 'translation' of MacDiarmid's Lallans-inflected poem 'The Bonnie Broukit Bairn':

Shookàr Mooklò Chàv
after Hugh MacDiarmid

Mars is lacshòo in har lalò,
Venus in charyalò kesh diklò,
O poorò Moon khelèl sovnalò peri,
Their starry horatibà chalalìparipè,
Sparin' khanchik, na dyooshyoondinè
Earth, dàle shookàr mooklò chàv!
– *But ruv an' in àsoos you'll drown*
O sastò àshariba!

shookar: beautiful; mooklò: abandoned; chàv: child;
lacshòo: fair, handsome; har lalò: crimson, deep + red;
charyalò; green; kesh: silk; diklò: Romani shawl; O
poorò: the old; khelèl: shake (v.); sovnalò: golden; peri:
feathers; horatibà: talk; chalalìparipè: load of nonsense
(chalalì: foolishness, paripè: load); khanchik: nothing; na
dyooshyoondinè: no thought; dàle: you dear! (voc.); ruv:
weep; àsoos; tears; o sastò àshariba: the whole wrestling
match.

I sometimes forge poems in Angloromani but I have also made
poems using other Romani dialects. I have reforged poems using
Romani from specific places and periods of the past, trying my
best to ensure the speech (much of which might no longer be
spoken) reflects both context and history. What I have learned
is that the porosity of Romani resembles the porosity of another
cunning language, English, which also borrows from other
tongues, thrives through dialects and idioms, and makes natural
alterations and reclamations.

How does Romani work on the ear? Mercifully for non-speakers, Romani words are pronounced exactly as they appear. In part, the language is highly onomatopoeic. The poet Ilija Jovanović – who writes in the Gurbet Romani dialect – calls it 'our singing language'. Romani offers qualities of cadence and linguistic energy that go beyond meaning. Its performance on the ear echoes Robert Frost's notion of 'the sound of sense'. Audience members have remarked to me at literary festivals that they have understood my Romani poems by simply hearing them aloud.

For me and for other Romani-speaking writers such as the artist Damian Le Bas, Angloromani is a language into which we travel quite naturally because it is the dialect of our tribe. For me, it offers an opening between fields of language. Romani contains many words and phrases from other languages because language is absorbed as it is travelled through. I believe Angloromani identity works in a similar way, unresolved and open – half-in and half-out of majority cultures. I do not view myself, or identify myself as a Romani artist. To paraphrase Nabokov, identity with all its selective apparatus is more like art than unadulterated life. What I would say is that there is much to be said for travelling between languages, for leaving a trail of words or images so that others might follow, even though they may never quite understand the meaning or the journey:

Patrìn

or *pateran,*
pyaytrin, or *sikaimasko.*
The marker used by Roma
that tells others of their direction,
often grids of branches or leaf-twists or
bark-binds. Used for passing on news
using prearranged forms, patterns
or permutations of these. Yet
it also means a leaf or,
simply, a page.

Simply, a page
yet it also means a leaf
or permutations of these
using prearranged forms, patterns.
Bark-binds used for passing on news,
often grids of branches or leaf-twists
that tell others of their direction.
The marker used by Roma:
pyaytrin, or *sikaimasko,*
or *pateran.*

Acknowledgements

The poems quoted in this essay are from my *The Invisible Kings* (Carcanet, 2007). I recommend *The Dialect of the English Gypsies* by B.C. Smart and H.T. Crofton, 1875 (reprinted by Bibliobazaar) and thank Damian Le Bas for alerting me to *Romani in Britain: The Afterlife of a Language* by Yaron Matras (Edinburgh University Press, 2010).

David Morley
'Ballad of the Moon, Moon'
(After Lorca)

Ballad of the Moon, Moon

El aire la vela, vela.
El aire la está velando.

A pettelengra boy whacks petalos on his anvil.
The moon slides into his smithy, bright as a borì.
The boy can not stop himself staring. The moon
releases her arms in flames of flamenco,
her sweet dress slipping from one shoulder.
'Nash nash, choon, nash nash, choon, choon.
If the Rom catches you he will splice your zi
He will smelt your soul for miriklè and vongustrì.'
The moon smiles, 'Chavvo, let me kur my kellipen.
By the cherris the gyppos come, they will find you
poggadi on the anvil with your biddi yokkers lelled.'
'Nash nash, choon, nash nash, choon, choon
Run for it, moon, run away, moon, fair moon.
I can hear hooves of my horse masters hammering.'
'Chavvo, muk me be. Don't pirro upon my pawni

ringi so rinkana.' The drumskin of the plains thrums
with hoof-strokes. The boy backs across the smithy.
Horse masters hove through the night tree
a forest in slow motion, bronze and dream.

Bronze and dream are the Roma, their eyes sky-high,
their gaze lances through walls of world and smithy.
But the moon dances her prey to the snare of a mirror.
She hauls the pettelengra o kolè dyoonaste to the pliashka.
The gypsies ride at her trailing veils, her mokkadi doovàki.
The wind whips by, wraps the moon in her purlènta.
It wraps that bride, the moon, the moon, *barval, bevvali.*

Romani – **pettelengra**: blacksmith; **petalos**: horseshoes;
borì: bride; **nash**: run away!; **choon**: moon; **Rom**: Romanies;
zi: heart, soul; **miriklè**: necklaces; **vongustrì**: rings; **Chavvo**:
boy; **kur my kellipen**: do my dancing; **cherris**: time;
poggadi; broken; **biddi**: tiny; **yokkers**: eyes; **lelled**: locked
up; **muk**: let/allow; **pirro**: tread; **pawni**: whiteness; **ringi**:
dressed; **rinkana**: spruce; **o kolè dyoonaste**: beyond, in the
other world; **pliashka**: Romani ceremony before wedding;
purlènta: silk headkerchief; **mokkadi**: dirty; **doovàki**: veil;
barval, bevvali: wind.

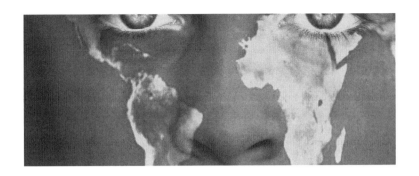

Parraruru
Two poems
Translated, the first from the Yindjibarndi,
the second from the Ngarluma by
Shon Arieh-Lerer

Parraruru, 1889–c.1975, was a leading poet and storyteller
of the Western Australian Pilbara Desert. Throughout the
1960s he was one of the main Yindjibarndi and Ngarluma
language informants of Von Brandenstein, who was working on
dictionaries and recordings of the oral literature of the Pilbara
languages. In addition to being one of the most prolific bards of
the region, Parraruru was a leader of his people as well as a feared
mawarnkarra (magician).

The Men of the Past

A long time ago men travelled in warring bands,
the men of the past. They travelled to slice and spear each
   other.
They killed each other, the men of the past.

Warring bands rose and travelled and sliced and speared.
They killed each other.
Some left the bands in fear, others as dead men.
They threw boomerangs at each other, they threw spears,
the men of the past. They travelled to other lands,
in warring bands they travelled, slicing and spearing.
They travelled to kill each other.

They did not bury the men they killed. They left each other
    lying
dead out in the open. They left each other dead everywhere,
the men of the past. If the men ever sat up and talked to one
    another at night,
an enemy would spear them. So they were always silent.
They lay down to sleep early.
The men who went on to kill in other lands eventually
    returned
to the first land where they killed, to slice and spear and
    keep killing there.
They travelled to other lands,
in warring bands they travelled, slicing and spearing.
They travelled to kill each other.
Everywhere, the dead lay out in the open.
Don't bury them! Let them lie!
Then every man of the past returned to his land.

Tarda Tells the Moon

The new moon rises.
The new moon rises in the west.
An old woman sees him rise, lights a torch and incants to the
    moon in the west:

This time you will not become a full moon,
for you will eat none of our food.
None of our meat! No, you will eat nothing!
The meat is for us, for me.

The lizard is for me.
The kangaroo is for me.
The emu, for me.
                              Nothing for you!
Turkey for me.
Fish for me.
                              Nothing for you!

All meat is for us, for me.
All food is for me! Not you!
Every fruit is for me! No fruit is for you!

You used to never eat at all – you were only the moon, alone,
    lighting the land.

I have to cook in the ashes.
Meat, seeds, kangaroo, lizard, emu, bustard – I have to cook
    these in the ashes.
You don't!
You are only there to light the land. But I have to cook meat
    in the ashes.

We must eat our meat well cooked, well cooked in the ashes.
And we cook our seeds in the ashes too – all seeds,
Wajurru pods and runner beans, we cook them in the ashes.

You will have nothing!

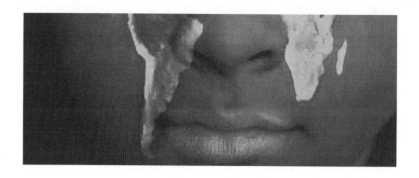

Nancy Campbell
'The hunter teaches me to speak'

The hunter teaches me to speak

I place my fingers round his neck and feel
his gorge rise – or is he swallowing
his tongue? He wants to teach me the word
for 'welcome'. Suddenly, he's trembling:
his larynx rumbles, then his breath is gone.
He asks me to remember those vibrations,
and, anxious as a nurse who takes a pulse,
touches my throat to judge its contortions.
Will I ever learn these soft uvulars?
I'm so eager, I forget that the stress
always falls on the second syllable.
My echo of his welcome is grotesque.
He laughs, an exorcism of *guillemets*,
dark flocks of sound I'll never net, or say.

Note

The influence of traditional orality still pervades Greenlandic culture. When my neighbours on the small island of Upernavik began to teach me Kalaallisut (Greenlandic), the lessons rarely involved written instruction. While other Eskimo-Aleut languages use the Inuktitut syllabary, Kalaallisut's polysynthetic words have been assigned the Roman alphabet, which does not accurately convey either its complex pronunciation or its silences. When it is spoken, many suffixes are uttered so softly that an untrained ear cannot hear them. Other methods, beyond spelling and sound, must be used to explain the form of the words.

The speaking of Kalaallisut became a political gesture in Greenland during Danish colonisation, which began in the eighteenth century. In 2009 Greenland achieved a degree of autonomy with the establishment of self-rule, and once again Kalaallisut became the official language of the nation known, in its own words, as Kalaallit Nunaat. But government recognition does not guarantee survival. In the same year, the United Nations culture agency designated Kalaallisut 'vulnerable' and predicted that Avanersuaq and Tunumiit oraasiat, the North and East Greenlandic dialects, would disappear within a century. Qavak, a South Greenlandic dialect, is already extinct.

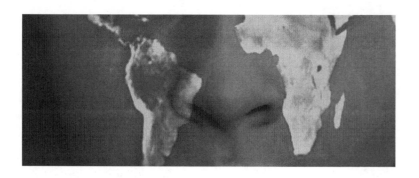

Ned Thomas
From Minorities to Mosaic

It is just as well that in 'Little Gidding' Eliot's interlocutor, impelled 'to purify the dialect of the tribe' is a 'familiar compound ghost' who must at the very least have Virgil's Latin and Dante's Italian as well as Eliot's English in mind. The association of *minority languages* alone with *dialect* and *tribe* would otherwise be ringing alarm bells. Twenty-five years of working with European minority language-groups, including my own, the Welsh, have made me over-sensitive to the terms used. There are no absolutely neutral ones. The French state prefers *langues régionales* since to speak of a minority in France suggests conflict. Basques and Catalans, when speaking French, prefer *minorisée* to *minoritaire* so as to emphasize that they are not minorities by virtue of some natural law but have been minoritized by the structures of state power. Numbers count but are not what define the minorities. Catalan-speakers are more numerous than Danish-speakers, Welsh-speakers outnumber Icelandic-speakers by nearly two to one.

Where once there was a clear distinction between *official* languages and the rest – often degraded to the category of *dialect* or *patois* – now one can find varying degrees of co-officiality on defined autonomous territories within the state. *Lesser-used languages* was a clumsy English translation of *langues moins-*

utilisées, the European Commission's attempt to find a neutral term that has now largely been overtaken by the Council of Europe's *regional or minority languages.* These include cross-border minorities – those who speak the language of an adjacent state but have minority-language status in their own states – such as the Finland-Swedes, or Hungarian-speakers in every country bordering on Hungary. These have their problems too, but not always the same ones as the free-standing minorities.

In continental Europe the distinction between long-established autochthonous languages and recent immigrant languages is well understood. Speakers of immigrant languages have different aspirations and a home territory elsewhere. But this has been less understood in the UK where *minority-language* has often conflated Scottish Gaelic and Welsh with Bengali and Gujarati, to nobody's benefit; but more than a decade of devolution and the most recent Welsh Language Act is fast changing that perception.

In the cultural and literary spheres – and this is particularly true of the Celtic languages because of the antiquity of their literature – majority cultures have often found it possible to romanticize and discriminate at the same time. The classic text for Welsh is the opening passage of Matthew Arnold's lectures *On the Study of Celtic Literature* where the poet stands on the Great Orme at Llandudno. Looking east the view towards Liverpool is busy with commercial activity but a little prosaic. But looking West he sees 'eternal softness and mild light . . . Wales, where the past still lives, where every place has its tradition, every name its poetry and where the people, the genuine people, still knows this past, this tradition, this poetry, and lives with it and clings to it.' One can understand that what David Jones called the 'bland megalopolitan light' required as its obverse, a twilit Innisfree, an unchanging, poetic area of retreat and escape from what Arnold in 'The Scholar-Gypsy' called 'this strange disease of modern life'; but the implications of this perception for the living Welsh language were not good and the word *clings* is a signal of worse to come.

Arnold's lectures which led to the establishment of the (now endangered) Chair of Celtic at Oxford for the study of the ancient literature, went on to urge that 'the sooner the Welsh language disappears as an instrument of the practical, political, social life of Wales, the better, the better for England, the better for Wales herself. Traders and tourists do excellent service by pushing the English wedge further and further into the heart of the principality; Ministers of Education [and let us remember that Arnold was an Inspector of Schools] by hammering it harder and harder into the elementary schools.'

While few would associate themselves today with the violence of those images, the underlying perception of minorities and their languages as representing some ancient, ethnic essence, unchanging yet doomed to extinction, dies hard and is endlessly reproduced in the tourist images of most minority-language areas. The implied contrast is with a plural, open, developing civic and modern culture, often perceived as the universal culture (though always language-bounded), to which minorities may be interesting contributory currents. But *every* language is a cultural crossroads of some kind, not a cultural island, and that is where we come to literary translation.

For the last decade, the Mercator Institute at Aberystwyth University has housed two related literary translation projects. The first has been funded by the Arts Council of Wales, and promotes the work of Welsh authors (whether writing in English or Welsh) through translation into other languages. This involves making their work known in all possible ways and offering grants to foreign language publishers to cover some of the costs of translation. The operation is run on a shoestring but over the decade more than 350 titles have been translated, and though more of these are from an English-language original than from a Welsh original, some of the most translated titles were originally in Welsh. There is the problem of finding translators from Welsh, of course. The Galician, Basque and Catalan Governments are acting to overcome their similar problem by the support of academic posts in foreign universities.

Our project's original title *Llenyddiaeth Cymru Dramor / Welsh*

Literature Abroad has recently been changed to *Cyfnewidfa Lên Cymru* / *Wales Literature Exchange* www.walesliterature.org as we came to realize the importance of mutuality for all but the most powerful English-language publishers. The rest of us cannot expect interest in our literature unless we also show an interest in inward translation. As part of this shift *Tŷ Cyfieithu* /*Translator's House Wales* was set up as a partnership with the *Tŷ Newydd* Writers' Centre to bring writers and translators together in Wales. The translation and adaptation of Latin and to a lesser degree French texts into Welsh was a vast industry in the high Middle Ages and the Renaissance, but in the modern period, though there have been heroic efforts by individuals to translate from languages other than English, the Welsh publishing scene has shared the general British lack of interest in translated literature. We hope that in a younger generation things may be changing.

Most smaller European languages, whether state languages or those of the institutionally stronger minorities, have a similar organization to *Wales Literature Exchange*, and these, together with book fairs and literary festivals, are partners in the other literary translation project led by the Mercator Institute, *Literature Across Frontiers*, EU funded and now in its tenth year. Some of our earliest and continuing partnerships in this project are with other minorities, but over the years LAF has expanded to become a network of networks involving all but the largest European languages and increasingly involved in literary dialogue across the Mediterranean with Arabic-speaking and other Middle-Eastern peoples, not forgetting *their* minorities such as the Kurds and Amazigh. An idea of the scope and scale of LAF's activities can be obtained from its website www.lit-across-frontiers.org and that of its associated on-line literary review *Transcript* www.transcript-review.org

The entry of Eastern Europe into the EU and into LAF has been particularly positive for us in Wales. Slovenia, Czechia, Slovakia, Croatia, the Baltic countries and others are all nation-states which have come into existence relatively recently on the basis of their linguistic identity. As in the case of Wales, these are places where literary figures have played an important part in the creation and maintenance of national consciousness. Moreover, their level of economic development and the size of their cultural institutions means that they are not in an entirely different league from the stronger minority-language groups of Western Europe. All this creates a context in which we can breathe – and cooperate.

The image that we come back to time and again when looking for a way to describe this variety of compatible elements is the mosaic. Gradually the majority/minority dichotomy may be overcome, and literary translation will play its part in the process, but that time is some way off – and still a long way off for those institutionally weak minorities marginalized in centralized states such as France and Greece.

David Hart
'Seagulls'

Milorad Krystanovich came to Birmingham from Croatia in 1992, from the upheaval in that part of Europe, and after a few years made the transition from making poems in Croatian to writing and publishing in English. His latest is *Improvising memory* (Nine Arches Press, 2010). In recent years he has been in less than good health, and as a gift I had the idea of a poem of a meeting of gulls from his birthplace and from my own. The words were put into Welsh by someone I was at school with, Helen Wallis, for which thank you; the Croatian is by Milorad, and I am grateful to his close friends Cathy Perry and Martin Underwood for enabling this process.

Seagulls
for Milorad Krystanovich, June/July 2011

Here they are now, the seagull from Zadar
and the seagull from Aberystwyth
in Victoria Square in Birmingham
on the edge of the Town Hall roof.

Odakle si?
[Where are you from?]

Esgusodwch fi?
[Excuse me?]

Odakle si? Ti ne govoriš hrvatski?
[Where are you from? You don't speak Croatian?]

Cymro. Squawk beth bynnag, cael deall ein
gilydd rhywsut mewn Cymraeg-Croat-Brummie.
[Welsh. Squawk anyway, get through to
each other somehow in Cymraeg-Croat-Brummie.]

Ti znaš što trebamo ćiniti, moramo ići ravno
u dućan, i ukrasti paketić čipsa i brzo izići sa tim.
[You know what we do, we walk straight
into the shop and we steal a packet of crisps
and walk smartly off with it.]

Ie, ond dyn ni'n ysgubo lawr a dwyn brechdan
syth mas o law rhywun, yno ar y promenâd.
[Yes, but *we* zoom in and steal a sandwich
straight out of someone's hand, right there
on the promenade.]

Inače, kako se snalaziš u Birminghamu?
[Anyway, how are you finding Birmingham?]

OK, mae'n debyg.
[OK, I suppose.]

Našao sam pileću nogu u fontani jučer.
[I found a chicken leg in the fountain yesterday.]

Ces i ddau sglodyn reit wrth ymyl y Frenhines Victoria.
[I found two chips right next to Queen Victoria.]

U redu onda, imaj dobar dan.
[OK then, have a good day.]

Chithe, hefyd.
[You, too.]

(We are sorry to say that since the poem was written Milorad
Krystanovich has died.)

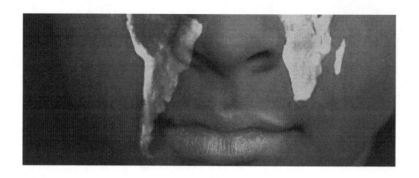

Noel Romero del Prado
Two poems
Translated from the Tagalog by
Jim Pascual Agustin

Noel Romero del Prado practises law in Manila in the Philippines. He has published a book of poetry, *Balat ng Dagat* (Salimbayan, Manila 1998).

Mayo Uno, Alas Singko

nakahahapis tingnan
ang dapat kong walisan

kung saan kanina'y
may dagat ng kamao
ngayo'y damuhang abo
ng mga polyeto

ipinagsama na ng hangin
ang ningas sa bawat talumpati
at hindi na matutupok
ang lahat ng naititik

nakahahapis pagmasdan
ang dapat kong walisan

May One, Five O'Clock

it makes me weep to see
how much i will have to sweep

where earlier
a sea of fists
now lies the ashen remains
of leaflets on grass

the wind has blown away
the fiery speeches
yet all those printed words
cannot be extinguished

it makes me weep to see
how much i will have to sweep

Revolution

A few more moments
and the whole archipelago
will be overrun with *gamugamo*:

The monsoon has arrived
and there is no escaping
the humming of their wings.

No one can say
where on earth they remain
through the long days of summer.

And who can say
where they may be led
by such fragile wings?

Are we not all surrounded by the sea?

Note: Gamugamo is the momentarily winged termite. The winged (or 'alate') caste, also referred to as the reproductive caste, are generally the only termites with well-developed eyes (although workers of some harvesting species do have well-developed compound eyes, and, in other species, soldiers with eyes occasionally appear). Termites on the path to becoming alates (going through incomplete metamorphosis) form a sub-caste in certain species of termites, functioning as workers ('pseudergates') and also as potential supplementary reproductives. Supplementaries have the ability to replace a dead primary reproductive and, at least in some species, several are recruited once a primary queen is lost. In areas with a distinct dry season, the alates leave the nest in large swarms after the first good soaking rain of the rainy season.

THE RIALTO

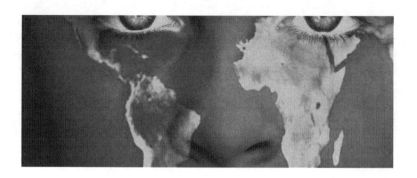

Jim Pascual Agustin
Four poems
Translated from the Filipino by the author

Jim Pascual Agustin writes and translates poetry in Filipino and English. He grew up in Manila in the Philippines during the Marcos dictatorship. He moved to Cape Town, South Africa in 1994. His early poetry books are *Beneath an Angry Star* (Anvil, Manila 1992) and *Salimbayan* (Publikasyong Sipat, Manila 1994). In 2011 the University of Santo Tomas Publishing House in Manila launched two of his new books of poetry, one in Filipino, *Baha-bahagdang Karupukan*, and the other in English, *Alien to Any Skin*.

Aso sa Tabi

Nagkukunwang basahan ang patay na
aso sa tabi ng tambakan. Isang pulgada
mula sa pusod ng sangsang

nananaginip ang buwan habang
nananalamin sa latang
maghapong tinubig-ulan.

Namumulaklak ng bangaw ang bawat bunton.
At sa dakong malapit
sa daan may batang naghahanap

ng kahit anong maaalagaan
kahit anong mapaglalaruan.

Pet

The lifeless dog beside the garbage dump
pretends to be a rag. A hand away
from the navel of stench

the moon dreams,
mirrors itself in a tin
filled by afternoon rain.

Each mountain of garbage blossoms
with flies. And close to the road
a child is digging around, looking

for anything to turn into a pet,
anything to play with.

From England

I was reading a book
from England
when something rattled
on the window. *Salagubang.*

Its chocolate-coloured wings
partly showing, it clung
to the tiny squares
of the screen. The moment

I came close, it slowly hid
its wings, like a secret.
Its body quivered,
as if panting

After a long journey.
Miracle of terraced fragility.
It climbed up
a few squares

Before it ceased and seemed
to stare at me and the book
from England in my hand.
That moment clung.

It felt as if the floor,
the window, the whole room,
everything was floating
in this ancient stare.

It quivered
and my hand grew cold.
I stepped out of the room,
quickly switched off

The lights and closed
the earth-coloured door.
I sat in some other part
of the house, in the living room

Or the kitchen perhaps. Tried
to read again
while knowing
it was waiting

In patience
for my return.

Salagubang – The common name for beetles in the Philippines. The one
mentioned here is found in mango trees. Filipino children use them as toys
in the rainy season when they fall off trees easily.

This Evening

this evening we offer to the moon
meals we left untouched

the coffins of sadness where we feasted
in the day have been thrown

upside down. slumped on the road,
our loved ones are waiting
for the light of the moon
to caress their lips, their remains.

should they speak, we shall listen.
we shall be all ears to their moaning

it may seem we are to blame
for all the suffering we bear.

no one shall wail, even
the children will be silent

like old people waiting for a visit.
this evening we will be offered to the moon.

Translator's note: the word 'labi' can mean 'lips' or 'remains' depending
on how one pronounces it. I have had to put both words in for the translation.

Century

I had seen them
before dawn dissolved
the moon:

Stirring coffee
without cups,
fingers with no nails
slowly tapping
legless tables.

Seated on the shadow
of the shadow of
kitchen chairs.

Whenever their mouths gape
petals break free,
murmur
of windblown leaves.

Just now,
at the sight of amber
on the acacia's side,
only now do I remember
those tales

Heroes embraced by death
yet will not rest

While the stench of war
lingers.

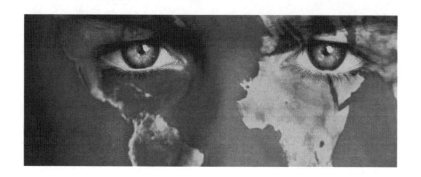

Luljeta Lleshanaku
Two poems
Translated from the Albanian by
Henry Israeli and Shpresa Qatipi

Luljeta Lleshanaku was born in 1968 and is regarded as the leading lyric poet in Albania. Growing up under house-arrest (her parents opposed the Communist regime) she was not allowed to attend university or publish her poems until the early 1990s, when she studied philology at the University of Tirana, subsequently working as a schoolteacher, magazine editor and journalist. She has published five collections and her first UK publication – *Haywire: New & Selected Poems* – is the recent Poetry Book Society Recommended Translation and coincides with her UK debut at the Aldeburgh Poetry Festival and a reading at the Southbank Centre in November.

23rd Aldeburgh Poetry Festival, 4-6 November 2011
www.thepoetrytrust.org

The Mystery of Prayers

In my family
prayers were said secretly,
softly, murmured through sore noses
beneath blankets,
a sigh before and a sigh after
thin and sterile as a bandage.

Outside the house
there was only a ladder to climb
a wooden one, leaning against a wall all year long,
ready to use to repair the tiles in August before the rains.
No angels climbed up
and no angels climbed down –
only men suffering from sciatica.

They prayed to catch a glimpse of Him
hoping to renegotiate their contracts
or to postpone their deadlines.

'Lord, give me strength,' they said
for they were descendants of Esau
and had to make do with the only blessing
left over from Jacob,
the blessing of the sword.

In my house praying was considered a weakness
like making love.
And like making love
it was followed by the long
cold night of the body.

Self-portrait in Silica

My portrait hasn't changed much.
My head still leans a little to one side
in the same way
as if asking for an apology.
Apology? For what?
Because I was in the wrong place at the right time,
or in the right place at the wrong time,
or both? Because I was present
when asked to be invisible?
Asked not to tap a spoon against my teeth while eating, not
    to dream out loud,
not to make smoke when I get burned, not to make suds
    when I wash,
asked to remove my feathers when I crumble
when the elastic breaks and my soul lands between my feet
asked not to bother fixing it?
And believe me, life is light when you are invisible.
I followed the path I was told to follow.
Glass! First I was glass, full of curses, the elementary school's
    window
made visible by dust.
Then I was the glass of a monocle that one eye trusted and
    the other didn't.
Later, after I began to write, I became the thick glass
of a telescope
that revealed stars on the palm of a hand.
The eyes that peer through me still look tired,
and the stars, still millions of light years away.
I bear no false news, only a premonition;
my deception has distance.

Maybe someday, I won't be an invisible thing,
a winding border between two worlds.
I will have a voice, a colour, and be read on rainy days
well aware that a timid nod to a photographer
is merely an alibi.

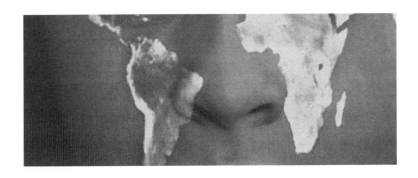

Yorgos Soukoulis
'Rise'
Translated from the Arvanitika by
Peter Constantine

In the Greek War of Independence, waged from 1821 to 1832 against the Ottoman Empire, many of the foremost freedom fighters were Arvanites. There was the legendary commander Markos Botsaris, and General Tzavelas, who was to become Prime Minister of Greece, the great Admiral Miaoulis, and General Kriezotis, commander of the forces of Euboea – to name a few. They spoke Arvanitika, one of the ten languages native to Greece that are listed today by Unesco as severely endangered.

The deeds of the great Heroes of '21, as these freedom fighters are called in Greece, are very present in people's minds today. But as Yorgos Soukoulis' Arvanitika poem *Grounni!* (Rise!) testifies, new generations have turned their backs on the ancient language, culture, and great Arvanitic deeds that are part of Greece's heritage. The woman of Souli who asks the poet 'Moua, pse me kharove?' – Why did you forget me? – is one of the women who took part in the 'Dance of Zalongo', a mass suicide of Arvanite women and their children in 1803. Trapped in the mountains of Zalongo in northern Greece by the advancing Ottoman army, they jumped to their deaths.

ΓΚΡΟΥΝΝΙ

Πάσσι νιέ νίντερε, ντιέ μπρέμα.
Ισ' νιέ γκρούα, μέ νιέ σσι τ' έγκιρε.
Μπάι μέ ζερβένε ντόρε, ντιάλινε ντ' αγκαλέ,
εδέ μέ τ' ντιάθετινε, νιέ δικόπε θίκε.
Μ' βισντόι μέ νιέ φιτίρε, τσ' τ' φρικιτόν,
εδέ μ' θά, μούα ψέ μ' χαρόβε;
Ε βισντόβα μέ φρίκε, εδέ μέ απορί ε πίειτα,
Τσίλια γιέ τί, ντίκου τ' κάμε πάρε.
Γιάμε νιέ γκά ατό, τσ' νιέ ι χούαϊ
μ' βού μέ μπογιέ, ντέ νιέ πλιχούρε
πρ' τ' μ' σιόχενε, ατά τσ' ο' βίνιενε
ψέ κίτα τάνετε, μ' χαρούανε,
παστάι μ' βιρβίνε, εδέ νάνι ντούανε τ´μ' κάουνινε.
Πό τί, ψέ μ' χαρόβε;
Ο γιέσ εδέ τί, νιέ γκά ατό, γκράτε ε Σούλιτε
τσ' πρ' τ' σπιτόνιτε τιμίνε γκά οχθρότε
ριμπίετε ντιέλτε τούαϊ, ντ' αγκαλέ,
εδέ ντίκου κιντούαρε, κέ σιντέτε κόσμι ι καιμόιτε,
εδέ ντίκου λιούαρε, ατέ βάουενε ε Ζαλόγγουτε
ού βιρβίτε μπάσκε μέ ντιέλτε, γκά σκιμπίνιετε,
εδέ σκρούαιτιτε, τ' μάδενε θισί εδέ ιστορί.
Γκράτε ε Σούλιτε ε Ζαλόγγουτε, γκρούννι.
Λίνι γκιάκιρατε τσ´ ντέρδτε, κονίσμε ντ´σκιμπίνιετε
πρ' τ' φάλενε, τ' πά λείτουριτε τσ' αρούνε.
Μίρι ντιέλτε, τσ' νάνι γιάνε μπίνε τρίμα,
εδέ βιρβίνε λιά, μπ' λιά γκά ρέτε, πρίζε ντ' ίλτε
πρ' τ' δινίσετε τ' ού σιόχε, χέπ κόσμι
εδέ λίουανι, νιέ χέρε μέτα, ατέ βάουενε ε Ζαλόγγουτε,
εδέ φιρτίενι, κιτίατε παλιοκόσμιτε
σά βιλιένε, τιμία εδέ λεφτερία
τσ' σπαγγούχετε, μέ γκί,
βέτιμε μέ γκιάκε, εδέ θισί
Γκρούννι, γκρούννι, ΓΚΡΟΥΝΝΙ.

Rise

I had a dream last night,
I saw a woman with wild eyes,
in her left arm she held an infant,
in her right hand a double-edged sword.
She glared at me and said,
'Why have you forgotten me?'
And I asked in wonder,
'Who are you? I know I have seen you somewhere.'
'I am one of the women a foreign man
captured with paint on a canvas
so that I can be seen by generations to come.
My own people have forgotten me,
cast me aside, and now seek to bury me.
But you? Why did you forget me?'
'You must be one of the women of Souli
who, to keep your honour from the enemy,
took your children in your arms
and singing 'Farewell, poor world',
and dancing our ancient dances,
threw yourselves and your children from the rocks,
writing sacrifice and history.
Women of Souli and Zalongu, rise!
Leave the blood you shed as icons on the rocks
so that our unborn generations can pray to them.
Take your infants, now grown, and fly high into the air,
above the clouds and between the stars
so all the world can see you,
and dance once more our ancient dances,
and show this world of misery the worth of honour
and freedom that can only be bought with blood and
    sacrifice.
Rise, rise, rise!'

**For a further note on the poet and his language see _MPT_ 3/15,
pp. 72-3.**

Afzal Ahmed Syed
Five poems
Translated from the Urdu by Nilanjan Hajra

Afzal Ahmed Syed is a product of the violent partition of the Indian subcontinent – one of the disastrous consequences of calculated British colonial policies. This entomologist poet, who was born in 1946 in undivided India, spent his early youth in what was then East Pakistan and witnessed the violent birth of a third country, Bangladesh, in 1971. For higher studies he moved to Beirut and experienced relentless Israeli bombardment of the city. Syed has finally settled in Karachi, Pakistan, a nation that has lumbered from one military dictatorship to another till as recently as 2008. Syed is one of the finest contemporary Urdu poets.

Urdu is a young language, which emerged in India in the 13th century AD. Scholars generally credit Vali Dakkani, a late 17th-century poet, for putting Urdu poetry on the literary map of India. Mirza Asadulla Khan Ghalib (1797–1869) was the first great Urdu poet.

Going by the calendar, Ghalib's 'In love my being got the fun of life / got the cure for pain, got a pain panacea-less' took some 150 years to be transformed into 'Love is not a visible sign/ Which could help identify the dead' in the hands of Syed.

Over these 150 years, besides exploring love in its myriad

hues, Urdu poetry has also been deeply political. This has been largely because the finest Urdu poets since Ghalib were in one way or another part of the resistance against the British colonial brutalities unleashed on the Indian subcontinent's 'beastly people with a beastly religion', to take a snatch from Winston Churchill.

Yet at the same time almost all the major Indian littérateurs of the period were deeply influenced by British education via which they came into contact with the rich intellectual discourse of the West.

The Urdu poets of the time were no exception. The two most important Urdu poets of the post-Ghalib era – Muhammad Iqbal and Faiz Ahmed Faiz – were eminently well versed in British and other varieties of Western thought. Being born and brought up during the colonial period, in their writings, they, on the one hand, rejected the unjust social order, and on the other, nurtured grand dreams about what a free society should be.

But not Syed. Be it Iqbal's dream of a just, egalitarian, pan-Islamic society, or Faiz's dream of a socialist society, none of them has any remnants left in today's Pakistan.

It is from within such history that Syed's poetry has emerged. Not surprisingly his collections bear names such as *History Arrogated*, *The Camp of Darkness* and *Death Sentence in Two Languages*. At the same time, Syed is very well exposed to Western thought and culture. Many of his best poems are in the collection titled *Rococo and the Other World*.

Radically different from the rich heritage of Urdu literature, the arrival of Syed marks a watershed in the history of Urdu poetry.

If I could remain in anyone's memory

Winter has arrived
The notice to supply woollen blankets to the prisoners is out
   again

Nights have changed
Their length, breadth and weight
But every night I keep dreaming
Of being caught while slipping through the bars

During the change of seasons
The time that couldn't be caught in any measurement
I read a poem

This poem was penned by my brother as he went to a war
He didn't return

But then I am more responsible than he was
I want to live till my time runs out

I know
The machines are hungry
And the dogs unfed

I know
How naïve are the snow and the clouds
And the hills
So helpless
I know
Those who live in the hills
Are very poor
And winter makes them poorer

Very few words can be written on the walls in monsoon
But then the winter is here
If I could have remained in someone's memory
In the memory of that girl, for example,
Who cries reading my poems
Something could have been written on the wall about
    releasing me

I know
My poems will remain unheard
I know
My heart
Imprisoned within floors and walls far cooler than this place
Will never be released on bail by anyone

I know
By the time the woollen blankets are supplied
The winter would have gone

I don't care for that white flower . . .

I don't care for that white flower
Which with a kiss you could turn red

A star falling apart in the sky
Or a boat sinking in the sea
With which one of these
Should I keep company
Your eyes
Or your heart
Didn't give me a hint

Mingling the din of the city
With the silence of my heart
Why did you compose your music

Why did you try to etch on fire
Your name
When your fingers are not made of diamonds

After the fire breaks out
It sinks in
What a stranger is the rain
And how distant is the sea
It becomes difficult to dream
That far away
Near our home
It must be snowing

I don't care for that dream
Which breaks while changing sides

I don't care for that snow
Which, dancing barefoot,
We can't turn red

Love

Love is not a visible sign
Which could help identify the dead

By the time you could detect love
The van must have left
The van which carries those bodies
Over which no one has any claim

Perhaps on the way
It went past your vehicle
Or perhaps you didn't take that road
By which
Those killed in love are usually taken

Perhaps the time required
To detect love
You had spent over some unavoidable chores

Time was laid on a stone slab
And the white linen
Drawn up to the limit of waiting
Must have been changed before you could finish your chores

Perhaps you didn't have
Any casual leave
Nor any dream
To identify love

By the time
You could touch love with your hands
That van must have left
Which carries away those dreams
Over which no one has any claim

Your fingers . . .

Your fingers
Didn't throw flying kisses
To the person sinking in the swamp
Nor did they shut the eyes
Of the dying man

The knots
That your fingers could so easily have untied
You cut them
With a dagger
That was used for human sacrifices

Wherever your fingers pass by
A shade remains
Of what was once a tree

Your fingers
Look beautiful in the shade
And you
In darkness

In darkness
There is a wounded bird
Whose cage
Your fingers will never open

If we didn't sing

We know the meaning
Of the life
That we are living

We know the weight of those stones
Which because of our carelessness
Have changed into things
To whose beauty
Our lives have added nothing

We felt our hearts
In flowers meant for decking the altar
At a time
When we
Were walking in a procession of wounded horses

Defeat is our god
We will worship it after death
We will die like a person
Who died in great pain

Life would never have known
What we expect from it
If we didn't sing

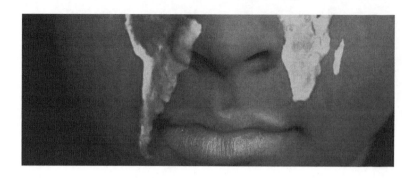

Hubert Moore
'Whistling back'

Whistling back
(*for Nasrin Parvaz*)

My neighbour keeps a quail
inside a shed (in solitary

confinement in Iran,
you used to tap out messages

on your next-cell neighbour's
wall). We're left alone

for hours, this quail and I,
caged up, well, I'm fenced off,

(and wait for a response), and so
it's no surprise that when

it whistles out its call
(you're never sure, you said,

your next-cell prisoner
might be planted there, to

listen, to entice), I whistle
back to it in Quail

as nearly as I can:
the little stutter, then

the full-blown upward-tilting
hoot. I hoot quite well,

I even know the Quail
for 'solitary' and 'I'.

Shamshad Abdullaev
'Voices'
Translated from the Russian by Alex Cigale

Born in 1957, in the Fergana Valley, Uzbekistan, Shamshad Abdullaev, winner of the Andrei Bely Prize for 1993, was awarded a Yeltsin Fund grant (2007) for his book of poems, *The place coming to mind.* His poems and essays have appeared in numerous journals, including *Znamya, Volga, Mitin Journal,* and *Zvezda Vostoka,* where he was poetry editor from 1991–1995. He is the leading figure of the so-called 'Fergana School', which he characterizes thus:

1. An orientation toward Mediterranean and, in part, American poetry.
2. A hybrid style, with one fixed variable – that the somewhat simulated, adapted components create a unified original.
3. Concrete landscape markers, the scorched southern world and along with it the hermeticism of 'southern' poetics; that is, through today's unconscious literary priorities, a certain cosmopolitan admixture of echoing illusions emerges, flooded by the sun.
4. An effort to carry the description of an object to the limits of naturalism within a generally unreal mood; and, simultaneously, in some instances it is possible to decipher

the following principle: the more alien the subject, the more
refined the method.

5. A turn toward the characteristic melancholy of late
    romanticism, expressed in a contemporary language, replete
    with scepticism and uncertainty.

6. Anti-historicity and opposition to social reality, fear before
    the instrumentality and totality of narration, a particular
    depressive lyricism and meta-personal obstinacy, not
    permitting an author of the 'Fergana School' to simply live
    life and each time distancing him from the meaning of
    events – this is why ethos in our texts recedes into shadows,
    fades into the background.

7. And lastly. We do not possess our own publications, our own
    journals, our own readers and are obliged to make peace with
    a diffuse presence (publication in Russia, abroad) for others,
    for another culture.

Shamshad Abdullaev, Fergana, 1998

Voices

That evening I was reading 'The Revolt of the Masses',
just as they were in those very hours
setting houses on fire. They say
an old woman ran out in flames, trying
to get out of the room (on her back – a starving red beast –
the fire as though feeding) but someone shot her in the head
and raced on further after human meat,
and this wound – like a third eye – reproachfully
gazed at the evil glow of the sky, already not discerning
the threat of the moaning redness, in which she herself
is rapidly dissolving, as though such were possible:
look upon this and forget yourself. And the earth, covered
    with asphalt,

rushed off, running away in a panic from the enraged crowd.
We had come across something similar in films,
either Vajda's, or perhaps Rocha's, and someone said:
he is trying to prove that History does not cleanse,
that it repeats itself and thirsts for blood, a flood of blood,
which does alas cleanse us, but only temporarily.
History – for this time, an undistracted and yawning
    bookishness,
gallingly descends from the screen and crumples our earthly
    Eden.
Now I know more about this than I would want to. I stood,
you stood off to the side, but in the neighbourhood barely
even a single side remained, delineated by death.
The corners of the houses and the streets were killed,
    badmouthed,
by their own betrayally precise respectable-trustworthiness.
The semis and buses screamed desperately, exactly as though
    being led to slaughter.
And only the streetlight was blinking without cease, nearly
    beside himself,
pretending to be a streetlight, and everyone
left him alone.
Was it always so? Who would say? Well, wise men.
'Here I am, my Lord, standing before you.'
We, we who daydream about the second, about the third
    Woodstock, of the kingdom of love . . .
Be silent.
There lay cremated scarves, fragments of dishes, scraps from
    carved lumber,
a maimed doll, a bra, dental implants,
a canary, dried to ashes, orphanhood, silence.
He (they) spoke very softly, as though speaking
caused him pain. When a ghost appears
it is immediately clear: it does not exist, it flickers. But this
    is something else,
here ghosts do not lie.

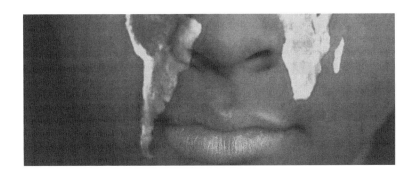

Itzik Manger
Four poems
Translated from the Yiddish by
Murray Citron

The first two, 'Suggestion' and 'At Every Morning's Light', are translations of translations. When Manger moved from Rumania to Warsaw in the early 1920s he put out a collection of folk songs which he had translated into Yiddish from various languages, called *Felker Zingen*. A number were Gipsy songs. These are two of them. In a short foreword Manger says that his approach was not scholarly but aesthetic, and that he not only translated but reworked the poems in the collection.

Later Manger wrote a lot of poems with Gipsy themes or characters. He evidently sensed an affinity between the Gipsy culture and his own Ashkenazi culture. In 'The Little Gipsy' the boy speaks of his own sorrow as a wanderer with only his fiddle, but also of the feelings of a wandering Yiddish poet with only his talent.

The golden peacock in 'Birth of the Poem' was a traditional symbol of Yiddish creativity in Eastern Europe.

Suggestion

The streamlet murmurs behind the mill.
A maiden stands and listens still.

Maiden, don't think the Dancer is cool.
He is greasy and sooty and always a fool.

Believe not the Traveller, pretty miss.
He always forgets his promises.

Even the Knight, with his pallid face,
Don't love him, he will bring you disgrace.

But choose the Klezmer and your heart will spin
With the joy of love in his violin.

A Gypsy song, from the Yiddish version in Itzik Manger,
Felker Zingen (Warsaw, 1930s), p. 75.

At every morning's light

At every morning's light
Just when the sun appears
I ask, where is he now?
And then I wash my face,
Not with fresh clear water
And not with gentle dew
But with my own hot tears.

A Gypsy song, from the Yiddish version in Itzik Manger,
Felker Zingen, p. 62

The Little Gypsy

I am a little Gypsy laddy,
Handsome as my Gypsy daddy,
Barefoot, hungry, sometimes wily,
And I live the life of Riley.
My mother never planned much for me,
Out on the steppe was where she bore me.
My father was hung and left us grieving
When he tried to feed us by going thieving.

Refrain:

Ah my fiddle, ah my violin,
Find where their hearts are, play my sadness in.
Ah you friend of mine,
Who knows more than you
That always, always,
Blood is red, and wine.

My legacy is my father's fiddle,
And on it I play 'Diddle Diddle'.
Whoever listens to it hears
My mother's grief, my sister's tears.
When my father to his death was driven
His violin to me was given,
With the melody it carried,
My father dead, my father buried.

I sing of being chased and hunted,
Past gates and under bridges shunted.
I am a little Gypsy laddy,
I learned to sing from my Gypsy daddy
Songs that are gloomy, songs that are funny,
They never cost a lot of money.
Whatever kind of song you order,
You can have my heartache for a quarter.

Original in Leichter, *Anthology of Yiddish Folksongs*, Vol. 7, The Itzik
Manger Volume, Hebrew University of Jerusalem, p. 26, with music.

Birth of the Poem

Young Gipsy girls, lovely daughters of the land,
Barefoot cousins of the winds and rains,
It's a long time since I met you in the country lanes,
In horse-drawn homes in a mysterious band.

In my young springtime years it was my way
To dream about my future and to start
And run to greet you with an open heart
And think on what will come, and ask you to say.

You murmured darkly. My open palm was clear.
The summer wind whispered in your black long hair.
The landscape thrilled with lilac, rose and green.

A peacock calling from the edge of sight
With moody wings diffused a golden light,
And I prayed my morning prayer on an old-time violin.

Norbert Hirschhorn
Two Jump Rope Songs

These poems are from my project to recompose Yiddish folksongs
into poems in English. Historically, some folksongs began as
poems, while some became poems adapted from the songs. (In
Yiddish *lid* means both song and poem.) The folksongs were,
in any event, often altered in passages from one person, time,
or country to another. Here I have tightened the verse, and
sharpened the rhythms to bring the songs to life in English.

A zun mit a regn, di kale iz gelegen,   Lady wid a baby
Vos hot zi gehat? – A yingele.   Named him liddle Abie
Vi azoy hot es geheysn? – Moyshele.   Fed him bread and gravy
Vu hot men es gevigt? – In a vigele.   Drove the neighbours crazy
Vu hot men es bagrobn? – In a gribele.   Rocked him in a shoebox
    Till he died of chicken pox

Oy vey mutter,	Hey hey mamma
Di kats lekt di putter,	Cat's into the butter
Di hiner leygen di eyer,	Hens ain't laying eggs
Di kale geyt in shleyer,	Bride's got hairy legs
Der chosn geyt in talis,	Rich man wears a shawl
Bam kabtsn iz der dalis,	Beggar's got none at all
Di kinder zoygen di finger,	Children gnaw their fingers
Di vayber shtarbn far hunger.	Women die of hunger
	Hey hey mamma

Recompositions based on skipping rhymes used by Jewish children in Eastern Europe. The first by Mendele Moycher Sforim (1836-1917) cited and with translation by Ruth Rubin, *Voices of a People. The Story of Yiddish Folksong* (Urbana and Chicago: University of Illinois Press, 2000), p. 48. The second, author unknown, from Ruth Rubin's *Voices of a People. The Story of Yiddish Folksong* (The Jewish Publication Society of America, Philadelphia, 1979), p. 280.

Cameron Hawke Smith
Three versions from Sorley MacLean's
Dàin do Eimhir

These versions draw on the English translations (in 'plain prose', as he described them) by MacLean himself, the Scots verse translations by Douglas Young, and the notes in Christopher Whyte's edition (*Association of Scottish Literary Studies*, 31, 2002). Though I have tried to reflect the Gàidhlig formal assonance, these treatments are more concerned to convey the powerful visual imagery of the poems. For that reason I have severely compressed Dàin XXVIII and XXIX. The titles of both of these poems are lines from MacLean's translations.

Dàin do Eimhir LIV
Dawn

You were the dawn on the Cuillins
stillness of waters between the islands
the sun on his elbow in the stream of gold
the white rose that breaks the horizon

Shimmer of sails on the luminous frith
blue-green of the sea, the sky's electrum
new light shining in the braids of your hair
and the sun rising in your complexion

Jewel of dawn, jewel of night, your
tenderness, and your beautiful face –
though the day of my youthful morning
is pierced to the heart by a death-grey stake

Dàin do Eimhir XXIX
The mild mad dogs of poetry

In that white land beyond time
across the perfected snowfield
I see the faint trails
of poems I have not spoken

Wolves and wolfhounds
their tongues bloody in their muzzles
streak through the forest
pathways, making for the uplands

Their howling fills the rocky
places of my brain, their onslaught
across the sheer mountains
driving confusedly onwards

The mild mad dogs of poetry
in pursuit of the white hind
that thing of serene beauty –
your face, a quest without end

Dàin do Eimhir XXVIII
The poets in their white shrouds of art

If I had won your love
perhaps my poems
would never have taken
that high bare road
of timelessness, nor ever spoken
of your beauty from the mountain
heights, in the desolation
of their mournful cry

They will go naked
on the streets and join
the poets in their white shrouds of art

They will stand with them
around the open grave,
will have no joy

And though they are grey
and keep the funeral wake
when sunrise breaks
their rose will outshine the dawn

Peter Kayode Adegbie
'To the bones that weep'
Translated into Yoruba by the author

The struggle for the control of the Niger Delta has fascinated historians, anthropologists, journalists and Nigerian writers, poets and memoirists; the Niger Delta on the southeastern coast of Nigeria is a mesh of creeks and mangrove swamps filled with fresh and brackish water.

When oil was discovered there in the mid-1950s it was expected to make Nigeria develop into an industrialised nation – 'the giant of Africa' – but it merely compounded the problem of growth. Nigeria has declined from being an exporter of cash crops to heavy dependence on oil revenues; it is estimated that 90-95% of Nigeria's export earnings come from petroleum and petroleum products, which also represent 90% of its foreign exchange earnings and 80% of its government revenues.

However, oil and gas explorations run by the British/Dutch oil company Shell has had adverse effects on the Ijaws, Oginis, Itshekiris, Urhobos and other indigenous people that live in the region. The government admits that 'pollution has affected the atmosphere, soil fertility, waterways and mangroves, wildlife, plant life, aqua life, and has resulted in acid rains. Fishing and agriculture are no longer productive enough to feed the area . . . the population is prone to respiratory problems and partial deafness'.

'To the Bones that Weep' is the prologue to my novella in verse *The Prophet, The Pirate and The Witch*, a unique narrative contribution to this intriguing subject at a time when the region has become an ongoing trouble spot and flashpoint of conflict between Christian, Islamic and African traditional cultures.

To the bones that weep

I will sing to *Olodumare*, who made all things,
the tale aflame in the crucible of my heart.

I will pestle consonants and vowels in a rhythm
till idioms stir and begin to live. I will leap

as one intoxicated with the treasured wine
of the oracles. I will roar like Sango

the god of thunder whose axe sculptures
mountains in the sun. I will sing

of ancestral wells, I will sing of *Yemonja's*
breasts. I will sing of the ways

of *'merindinlogun'*, I will sing of the sacred
secrets of *Ifa*. I will sing of the wells

of knowledge now forgotten like roots
in Sahara sands. I will sing an elegy

of coastlands where bones weep. I will sing
of lands mined and shelled in oil, wasted,

so 'sweet and light crude' can flow, where
life bleeds and souls decay like seeds

planted in fetid soil. How long till I'm weary
of songs? How many more messiahs?

*   *   *

Who should bear the blame of ruined lives?
This pawn-play of masters who insatiably

contend on the oil-soaked chessboard of the dead
and dying, those without reprieve? Our

sacrifices are warm on clay altars, the blood
we shed thicker than oil in our mayhem

of lust for power and struggle for wealth, yet
the gods have not smiled. How long

will the land languish as souls sigh and youths
are spirited away to an eternity of agony

to lament their unfulfilled dreams. I will sing
for the living who envy the dead in five

hundred billion dollar bottomless black hole
greed, where youths wait in vain to live.

Olodumare, how long? We cover dead skin
with fine robes as marrow wastes in toxic

fumes that serpentine heavenward as bones crackle
in the heat, flesh sizzles and our tears fry;

how long shall we sing, bruised, crushed, throttled?
We grasp at pipes, till rivers of blood flow

with the devils' excrement – the oil that they seek.
I will cry like Job in Satan's smouldering furnace,

I will cry against the ravaging AIDS, the damaging
poverty, against the odious arrest of my song

in flaring gas, I will cry till aghast with deep rage,
till my tears irrigate this forlorn earth; perhaps,

ample tears will salve addiction to this opium of oil;
let me cry freedom, freedom for Niger Delta

– that cesspool where oil addicts shit and vomit,
yet insist on more. Let me mourn the graduates

and undergraduates out of the colleges, destitute,
jobless, destined to a bleak future; let me

voice the anxieties of civil servants pushing
the system, hobnobbing with conmen

hunting for scams; let me speak for desperate traders
on the fringes, tending their cancerous anger.

Shall we continue this song in the sun,
with muddied lingerie worse than

menstrual rags? Shall we dance with shamed
and tattered robes that tear in acid rains

that burn in Angola, Equatorial Guinea, Congo,
Gabon, and above all mother Nigeria?

Níbi tí Egungun ti Nsokún

Èmi ó korin ìtàn tí ó n'gbèrú nínú okàn mi sí Ólódùmarè,
tí ó dá ohun gbogbo. Èmi ó lu kónsónántì àti fáwèlì
bí eńi lu bàtá, títí àwon òwe yó fi dìde, tí won ó sì di alàyè.
Èmi yó fò śokè gégé bí òmùtí tí ó mu otí ebo òrìsà
ní àmupara; ohùn mi à sán bí àrá, bí ìgbàti Şàngó
oba kòso, eni tí ó nfi àáké gbé àwon òkè sínú oòrùn.
Èmi ó korin nípa àwon kanga àtijó, nípa omú Yemoja.
Èmi ó korin nípa àsírí ifá, nípa àwon ònà Mérìndínlógún.
Èmi ó korin nípa àwon kanga, ogbón ìmò àti oye
ti o ti di ohun ìgbàgbé, bii gbòngbò inú aginjù.
Èmi ó korin nípa àwon omi nlá, níbi tí egungun ti nsokún.
Èmi ó korin nípa àwon ilè níbi tí epo ròbì ti nsun jade wá,
èmi ó korin ilè gbígbéfún epo, ilè tí ó di yepere nítorí epo,
ilè tí a so di asálè kí epo ròbì lè maa sán níbi tí èjè tí nsàn,
tí okàn sì dàbí ilè ahoro bí èso tí a gbìn sí orí asálè.
Ìgbà wo ni ngó ko orin arò yí dà?
Orin kíko sú mi. Olùgbàlà melo ni à nretí?

                    *   *   *

Tani a ó dá lébi fún opòlopò èmí tí o ti sègbé?
Ní agbo eré àwon alágbára aye, àwon olójúkòkòrò
tí wón so èmí àwon ènìyàn di opón ayò àtaàta tán.
Àwon aláìbìkítà. Ebo titun ni a gbé sí oríta, èjè tí a ta sílè
ju epo ròbì tí a wà pèlú ìwànwara, eré àsápajúdé fún owó
àti ipò, síbè àwon òrìsà kò túraká síwa, ìgbà wo ni ilè
yó ké ìrora dà? Àwon okàn nmí ìmí èdùn. Àwon òdó
nlo ìrìn àjò àrè mabò lo sí ibi tí wón ndárò nípa ìgbésí
ayé tí kò ní láárí. Èmi ó korin fún àwon alààyè tó nwípé
ikú sàn ju èsín, ní ìlú tí dollar egbegbèrún tí bá wòbìà wolé,
tí àwon òdó ndúró láti gbérí. Olódùmarè títí di ìgbàwo?
A nfi aso àláárì bo àwò tí o ti dípetà, èmí nsòfò nínú èéfín
Ìparun, tó njó lo sí òké òrun, síbe, egungun wá sé nínú

òòrùn gbígbóná, ara njóná, ekún wa sì gbe, ìgbàwo ni a ó
korin dà, pèlú ìrèwèsì àti okàn tí a tè mole bí erin tegbó,
tí a lù bole, bí ení nlu olè. Èro epo di ohun àdìròmó títí
èjè fin sun bí omi odò pèlú ìgbé èsù, emi ó sokún kíkoro
bíi jóbù nínú panpé èsù; emi yó gbé ohùn mi sókè nípa
àìsàn AIDS, jejere bí ikán, nípa osì, àti nípa àwon tí ó
ntiraka láti pa mí lénu mó pèlú iná ìléru.
Èmi yó ké pèlú ìbínú nlá nínú ìdàmú mi, bóyá omijé ojú mi
yó gba ilè yí íówó àwon eni ibi tí nmu epo ròbì ní àmupara
bí otí. Jé kí ariwo mi kí ó máa dún pé ìtúsílè, ìtúsílè fún
     àwon ará
Delta, ní agbègbè ibi tí àwon tí nmu epo bí ení mu otí
     ngbonsè sí,
tí wón sì nbì sí, tí wón sì tún nkígbe pé àwon nfé si; èmi ó
     sokún
àwon òdó òmòwé, tí kò rí isé léhìn tí wón tí lo sí ilé ìwé gíga,
tí wón kò sì ní ìrètí ohun kóhun fún ojó iwájú.
Jé kí ohùn mí jé agbejórò fún àwon osìsé ìjòba, tí nfi ìdí
     gbòdí
pèlú àwon oní jìbìtì, èmi ó sòrò fún àwon olójà, àwon oní
     wóróbo
tí wón kò mo bi ojà nrè, tí ìbínú wón dà bíi ti iná ìléru;
sé kí á máa korin lo lábé òòrùn pèlú aso àkísà tí ó rírí
bíi aso tí obìrin fi se nkan osù, sé kí á máa jó lo pèlú aso ìyà
tí ó ya mó wa lára bí aso tí ojò iná to so di àkísà.
Ojò iná tí ó nrò ní Angola, Equitoria Guinea, Congo, Gabon,
Àti pàápàá ní ilè Nigeria.

Juri Vella
Poems
Translated from the Nenets by Katerina and Elena Zhuravleva

Juri Vella is a western Siberian indigenous poet who belongs to the tiny group of the Forest Nenets (circa 2000 people). But he is much more than only a poet, and probably poetry in his life occupies a minor amount of his time. Most of it goes to just living and surviving. Shortly before the end of the Soviet era in Russia, Juri decided to quit his job as hunter in a state farm and move with his family to the forest to be a reindeer herder and lead the traditional way of life of his people. Villages in western Siberia are purely a product of Soviet rule: nomads and semi-nomads were sedentarised between 1930 and 1950, and compelled to work for collective farms. Juri felt the call of the forest and the reindeer. Today, he lives mainly in camps he has built himself, in the company of his wife, sometimes one grandchild or another, and more than a hundred reindeer. He is the head of a huge family, four daughters, their husbands and their children, fed primarily by Juri. Work in the village, after 1991, is scarce and precarious. In the forest, he is sure to have meat and fish, to have his material needs covered and, morally, to work for his well-being and that of his family.

However, this does not come without permanent struggle: the territory he lives in is part of a huge oil basin that gives 80% of Russian oil. Oil companies are everywhere since the 1970s and they have no time for native populations or the natural environment. The oil drillers' mentality is to submit nature to their will. The indigenous peoples living in the forest – Khanty and Forest Nenets – are inconvenient because their mere presence interferes with the free exploitation of natural resources. Just living is thus an everyday fight for the survival of animals, people and nature, not only for today, but also for the next generations. When Juri finds free time, he writes poetry: his everyday life is what inspires him.

Eva Toulouze, Tartu, Estonia, August 2011

From 'The Spring Triptych'

The sky of different colours

Once a poor hunter opened up his smoky choom. Took a deep breath. The sky flew into the choom. It turned into wellbeing and happiness. It still lives there with the man.
(*from Granny Nengi's tales*)

I live under the coloured sky,
and the colours are so familiar:
the melancholy sky,
the tender one
that may be very fresh, but partly gloomy.
The merry sky that
may sometimes be so cold.
It can be elegant, but also playful.

The bright sky,
the red sky,
the kind sky,
as beautiful as a bride.
Defenceless as a child and strong.
The sky of yellow,
the sky of green,
the sky of blue, and of purple.
The sky may also be quick
or it may stand still.
It may be either loud
or very very quiet.
And high,
and low,
and dense,
and dry,
and sparse,
and wet.
Silvered.
Gilded.
Bluish.
It may be an official who swaggers,
or Nenets-like simple and so close.
My sky resides in the orange piece of glass
that my daughter carries in her hands.
The sky is set in the friendly open choom
that my Granny opened wide for you.
The sky is a panorama set in your window,
so spacious,
light,
without bars,
with a frame of azure,
with creaking shutters
and ox-eye daisies on the windowsill.
With your mother's face,
smiling as in a portrait.

The sky can lie down on the earth.
Or on the sea,
or on the tundra.
To rest after the hardest hunt,
or after fishing,
or after weeding.
The sky can be above the world
above the stars
above the suns
above the galaxies as well.
The sky may become as weightless
and as noiseless as a butterfly's wing
the sky can be . . .
But No!
No!
I know no other sky.
No!
It cannot become any other sky.
No!
It cannot become anything other than the sky.
My sky is of different colours
and you live under it too.

From 'Loneliness'

1.
Passing by white roofs,
the stove pipes of chooms,
the thin high smoke
of my stand-camp
you are shifting through in a hurry for
the places,

where rivers are not yet frozen,
the places,
where lakes are not yet frozen.
Why are you so delayed?
Winter has already overtaken you not only behind
but in front,
upward with lapping sweeps
a way paved by other flocks.
Your wings
are already ragging up snowy whirls
laboriously
painfully
they beat at my face,
and touch my heart.
What are the young screaming about?
What is it about?
What are experienced geese
bravely but worriedly chattering about?
After all, I hear their farewell song
not for the first time,
and I can't understand why
it fills me up with pain.
Why?
Perhaps today
I am like that delayed flock?
It is possible to take off now,
But tomorrow will be too late . . .

'From 'Forest Pains'

'My daughter, protect your banks, for the White Moss could increase joy in the reindeer's gaze, for the Red Squirrel could bring up its brood in a Cedar Hollow, for the Woman who is mistress of the Needle could always sew the White *Kissi* and White Mittens for her daughters and sons so that there would always be good snow under the Lucky Young Boy's skis, so that the Hard-working Young Boy's heels would always step fortunately . . .' These were the words of As-Eeky (an elder of the Ob) to his still-young Agan Daughter. (*From Grigory-Eeky's Festival song*)

The fourth pain

Oh, taiga!
There is no taiga, it was cut down.
Oh, my native land!
There is no land left,
it has been changed into metalled roads,
it has been changed into busy, harsh, open pits
it has been changed into stone suburbs.
Who can I address this to?
I who to my misfortune survive?
The rivers and lakes and seas
are full of oil.
And the antlers of my grandfather's last reindeer
with their skulls
have been taken for souvenirs.
Soon, perhaps, the lovers of the exotic

will get to me . . . ?
Oh, tundra!
Today I'm going to your polar space.
Oh-oh-oh!
That is all that remains of the tundra!
Let me get the last gulp of your fresh air
as a souvenir.
And as a souvenir
let me get the last gulp of pure sense.
Tundra!
Let me see only once
how the sun will lightly touch
your squinting eyes.
But before the very sunset
the tundra meets me
with a radioactive aurora
and poisoned acid rain . . .
Oh, horror!

From 'A Triptych Stained with Mazut'

1. A cloud in oil

Dedicated to the deeds of drilling master Pahomov's team
from Mirnins, who drilled object K-8 on the Povhov oilfield
near the Varyogan river and released waste products into the
river. This oilfield, along with others, was later called Lukoil.
    'Every spring during the flood a thick pellicle of oil
floated down the Varyogan river from the Povhov oilfield. It's
become hard for us to live . . .'
(*From the native people's statement to the Agan executive committee
of village Soviets, 1982.*)

There is
oil,
oil,
oil,
Floating down Varyogan river.
Boat, oar and nets are
saturated with oil.
If you disembowel a pike
the whole knife is stained with oil.
There is no place
to take water for a kettle.
Reindeer's legs are covered
with oil,
oil,
oil.
Someone runs out of a neighbour's place
with disastrous news to tell.
Even the crow's belly
is greasy.
The clouds in the sky
too have darkened.
There are oil blots
on the lap of the choom.
The black line
Has crossed my forest . . .
Little reindeer of my childhood
why are you crying so hard?
That smudgy face of yours
I'll wash with morning dew.

(Mazut is a form of low quality fuel oil peculiar to the former USSR.)

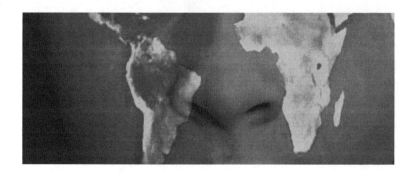

Saradha Soobrayen
From Ilois to Chagossian

'We, the inhabitants of Chagos Islands – Diego Garcia, Peros Banhos, Salomon – have been uprooted from those Islands…Our ancestors were slaves on those islands, but we know that we are the heirs of those islands. Although we were poor there, we were not dying of hunger. We were living free.'

(Petition to the governments of the United Kingdom and the United States, 1975. See David Vine, *Island of Shame*.)

'The Chagos islands are among the most remote in the world, situated in the Indian Ocean 1,200 miles northeast of Mauritius. They cover an area of ocean of 54,400 km2 and comprise many atolls, islands and submerged banks. Their land area is only 60 km2 with the largest island, Diego Garcia, being horseshoe-shaped and 14 by 4 miles. Human settlement on the Chagos Islands dates back to the mid-1780s when a French sugar and coconut plantation owner from Mauritius, or Île de France as it was then called, established a coconut plantation… After the defeat of Napoleon in 1815, the Chagos islands passed from French to British rule; 20 years later, slavery was abolished, followed by abolition of the leper colony. In 1828, there were 448 inhabitants on the Chagos islands with Diego Garcia containing more than half. As the population on Diego Garcia continued to grow, the other islands, Peros Banhos and Salomon, were also settled as the plantation owners began importing indentured labourers from India in the 1840s and 1850s. These new workers gradually integrated into Chagossian society and many of them, along with the Chagossians, converted to Catholicism. Many of the Indian labourers intermarried with the inhabitants thus becoming the ancestors of today's Chagossians.

(From *Stealing a Nation*.)

I first became aware of the illegal removal of 2000 Chagossian Islanders from the Chagos Archipelago when I watched John Pilger's documentary *Stealing a Nation*. Between 1971 and 1973 Great Britain and the United States exiled the entire population of the Chagos Islands. The islanders were forcibly removed, misled, and left to live in squalid conditions in Mauritius and the Seychelles, in order to make room for a joint UK/US defence base. At this time not only were the Chagossian people the original and rightful inhabitants of the Chagos Archipelago, they were also citizens of the UK and the colonies. This act of neo-colonialism particularly struck a chord with me as I have dual nationality with Mauritius and Britain and was appalled but not wholly surprised by the behaviour of my native lands.

The British Government secretly signed a military agreement in 1966 with the US leasing Diego Garcia for an initial 50 years for military purposes. A new colony was formed: the British Indian Ocean Territory. Diego Garcia is mid-way between Asia and Africa and has excellent anchorage making it an ideal spot for military intervention in the Middle East, Afghanistan and Iraq. More recently the military base Camp Justice on Diego Garcia was used for the transport of prisoners in the controversial Extraordinary Rendition program.

Despite having ancestry dating back to the eighteenth century, the Chagossian people were deemed to have not existed and were described by the UK Government as a floating population of migrant workers. The US Government was also complicit in maintaining the fiction within their own country and to the wider international community.

During the 1960s the pre-independence Government of Mauritius agreed to the detachment of the Chagos Islands for a fee of £3million and agreed to accept the islanders, who found themselves in abject poverty, starving, and dying of *Sagren*, a profound sadness. They were marginalized and discriminated against as an inferior people, a subset of Mauritian Creoles known as ti-kreol, the lowest of the low. A recent bill was amended this year in Mauritius to recognize 'Chagossian' as a specific and distinct community and ethnic group, thus replacing the commonly used term *Ilois* which vaguely suggests 'islander' and has evolved to be used as a form of insult.

On the 3rd November 2000 for the first time the Chagossian rights as a people were recognized by the High Court of London who ruled that 'the wholesale removal' of the islanders was an 'abject legal failure'. The current struggle for justice and the right to return to the Chagos Islands is now being continued through the European Court of Human Rights as well as the International Court of Justice in the Hague, led by the formidable Olivier Bancoult, Chairman of the Chagos Refugees Group.

The evolution of Chagos Kreol is clear evidence for the historical rights of the Chagossian people and is a living, breathing record of their colonial heritage. Chagos Kreol shares the influences of the mother tongues of slaves and indentured labourers: Tamil, Malagasy, Makhuwa and other Bantu languages of South East Africa. This melange of tongues has resulted in a distinct Kreol that differs from Mauritian Kreol and *Seselwa* Seychellois Kreol in its vocabulary and pronunciation. All Indian Ocean Kreol languages are understandable amongst Kreol speakers and share many features and yet Chagos Kreol has its own unique slow melodious accent, which many exiled Chagossians made great efforts to hide in order to avoid the harsh discrimination in Mauritius and Seychelles. According to David Vine, 'most Chagossians lost most of the distinct features of the language after over four decades in exiles'. As with all marginal identities seeking to define themselves, the status of Kreol dialects is fragile, unwritten languages being prone to absorb from their new surroundings as well as diminish with neglect.

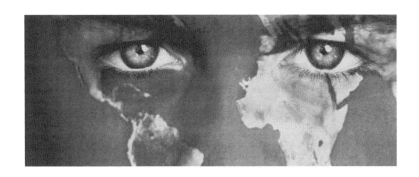

Saradha Soobrayen
'Who/Whose am I?'

Who/ Whose am I?

'What are you,
British? Mauritian?'

-*Non, non*

'What . . . *bet, ti-kreol?*'
-*Non*

'What arc you . . . *Sovage?*'

-*Non, non*

'No island, no homeland,
no right to return.'

-*Non la vie, non la vie!*

'Wait, wait, don't speak, think,
think twice, turn, turn your tongue
the wrong way round, lose it.

-Non, non

> 'Lose it, lose the taste for sound,
> the old, old songs: more than, more
> than patois, further, further than
> *lingua franca*, rounder, rounder,
> rounder than the belly of Africa.'

-Non, non

> 'What are you . . . savages?'

-Non, non

> 'Stupid little creoles?'

-Non,
-Nous Chagossienne nous . . . nous Chagossienne nous

Karen McCarthy Woolf
'Hoxton Stories'

My grandfather Charlie Robinson was born in Wilmer Gardens, Hoxton, east London in 1919 and died in Chichester in West Sussex on 1 January 2009. He lived in Islington until the early 1970s after which he joined many other working-class families in a mass exodus from sitting tenancies to council housing on the south coast, which paved the way for an urban gentrification that began in earnest in the 1980s. In just two generations the Hoxton of his youth in the 1920s and 1930s has transformed from a working class 'slum' brimming with overcrowded Victorian tenement blocks to the highly priced metropolitan hub of converted warehouses and nightclubs that it is today.

All through our lives he was a consummate storyteller and would enthral the family with his tales of growing up in East London between the Wars. He was working class, poor, and his mother, Florrie Robinson, taught him and his brothers to live on their wits. Being born within the sound of Bow Bells, as the saying goes, he was a bona fide cockney.

As such, he could speak cockney rhyming slang, although its usage is lighter in the stories I include here which are 'translated' from a tape he made with my mother a few years before he died. This is partly because rhyming slang would have been something he spoke with his peers, the boys he grew up with at the time.

In his 'translation' of telling the story to his daughters and grandchildren he has adapted the language to his audience: as we couldn't understand it, he used it less often. However, the syntax and vocabulary, characters and events are very much within the cockney vernacular and I have attempted to give a sense of the rhythms, cadences and nuances of his speech.

Most importantly, I have endeavoured to be faithful to his voice and the poems are almost verbatim reproductions from the tapes, although not quite, as I have used very loose rhyming couplets and terza rima rhyme schemes as a holding device. I have also allowed the stories to follow a more meandering arc in keeping with the oral tradition rather than the more formal structures of written narrative. There are some inconsistencies in the dropping and retaining of the letter 'h'. This is faithful to the speech patterns on the tape and reflects, I think, both a sense of aspiration in terms of social mobility, a natural proclivity towards dramatic emphasis and a desire to ensure that he was always understood. Throughout the process, every time I thought about changing something, I would usually defer to the original: he had the gift of the gab and there was little I could do to improve on it.

These 'Hoxton Stories' I hope not only will help to preserve a part of London's cultural history, but also record the spoken dialect of a particular tribe in a particular era.

Guy Fawkes Night

What you haf to imagine is a nah-sty, stinky
little street, with loads o' people, tinkers,

dockers, barra boys the lot, all living a dire
tedious existence. We never 'ad a care

in the world though poverty was rife,
because we was kids and we lived a life

in these tenement houses, flat top roof
tenements. Three rooms up top, three rooms

in the middle and three rooms down with a yard
where all you had to do was go to the kahzee.

Right, so it's Guy Fawkes night and these days
it don't carry the same sig*nif*icance that it had.

There was about eight kids including me
up on the roof, cos that was a place we'd play

and Jimmy Webb was a right little tea leaf
an' 'e'd been up Tom O'Leary's

which was a little general shop that sold fags
and sweets, rubber johnnies and also bangers!

So Jimmy's been in and grabbed an 'andful
of these crackin' fireworks, 'flashguns'

they called 'em and they woulda cost an 'alfpenny
each, and we're on the roof, got a little bonnie

goin', an we've tied about five o'these flashguns
into a little bundle and Jimmy's flung 'em

on the fire for a mo' so as to light the end,
and he's got this little bomb in 'is hand,

he coulda blown 'is whole bleedin' arm off.
Now Mrs Ruff, that's R-U double eff,

and she *was* rough, she lives downstairs. So Jimmy's
lobbed the bomb down the very first chimley.

Well, within seconds there's a huge great bang!
The chimley pot blew up, all the brickwork sang

through the air, missed us by inches as we rushed
to peer over the front. And there's Mrs Ruff!

She was covered in bleedin' soot from 'ead to foot!
Oh she was in a terrible state. We'd set fire to the cat

and her dinner'd been blown right across the kitchen.
But being kids we didn't know what we'd done,

so we all scuttled down our trapdoors that went
to our own compartments in that beau-ti-ful tenement,

with the air of innocence all over us.
When 'er three sons came 'ome from work, there was

Sammy Ruff, Billy Ruff and Bobby Ruff
and they *was* rough, two of 'em worked shifts

down the docks and one of 'em was a garman
and they were gonna kill the little bastards

that blew their mum right across the room
and spoiling their dinner when they got home too!

That was Wilmer Gardens, where we lived in 'Oxten.
So what d'ya reckon about that one, then?

Old Mutha Riah. Hoxton 1935

Testing testing testing! This is Charlie
Robinson here. Are you listening Mah-rie?

I've bin trying ta get this bloody thing ta forward.
I'm doin' this on a bleedin' Chi-neese recorder.

Well, as kids we all use-ta sing 'Old Mutha Riah,
pissed on tha fire!' and being old 'nd wise now I realise

we were 'orrible to 'er, but she was a freaky little
woman, she 'ad all disfigurement in 'er face, a muzzle

like a dog, hands like paws with little claws on 'em
and all the kids use-ta say she was half-'uman,

half-'ound, although whether that was really a fact
I don't know. She was an annual attraction

at the 'Ampstead Fair! They use-ta try 'nd lift 'er skirt
up in 'Oxten market to see if she had a tail or not.

I weren't one of 'em, but she use-ta beat 'em off
with 'er walking stick 'nd if you got a cuff

round the ear 'ole you knew all about it. Anyway,
one of my jobs when I worked on the railway

was to go to Broad Street Goods Yard.
It wasn't a very nice job, as usual it was a hard

grind and the thing was it entailed terrible hours.
That day we'd bunked in round the back o'the pictures

'cos we didn't make enough money selling 'orse
manure to a bloke who took it round the 'ouses for roses.

The picture was The Weeerewolf of London with
Fredric March as the werewolf. Scared me shitless

it did 'cos I 'ad a vivid imagination, like you got Mah-rie.
So I goes to work at night but they didn't want me

so we're coming 'ome, two or three lads, out late,
'nd we 'ad to walk from a place called Norton Folgate

which was the beginnin' of Dalston High Street
and we shot right through the market,

it was all dark and dismal and miserable and rainy
and the other two lads went on their way

'nd I started down Hobb's Place, a short cut,
forgettin' Old Mutha Riah lived thereabouts.

It was a full moon that night, when the werewolf
came out and anyway, I gets just past 'er 'ouse

and 'er bleedin' windeh shot up and she poked
'er horrible face through and shrieked:

'Whassa ti-iime!? Whassa ti-iime!?'
I didn't wait to tell 'er the time! I nearly died

of fright. I rushed 'ome fast as my legs could carry
me and lucky enough your nan, Florrie,

was up and about nursing a fag and a gin
and when I told 'er she couldn't stop laughing.

Pigeon racing

In Phillip Street there used to be a fella
who's name was Joey 'Ooker
an 'e was a very good pigeon fancier
'e had some lovely birds in a nice *dorm*er
an' everything. The idea of this pigeon racing
was that all the pigeon fanciers –
an' there was quite a lotta them – they mighta
fancied other things I don't know but – they use'ta
take the birds that was gonna be flown,
over to Epping Forest on a train
or somewhere round there, and time 'em off
and then put the bird's ring into a matchbox
and run it down to a place called Andretti's
in 'Oxten Markit, 'e use-ta take bets,
this Italian fella, had a big family,
'e was quite allright, use-ta sell ice cream.
Anyway, you used to 'af to 'ave three boys,
probably two or three that could run pretty
fast and he 'ad a bloke name a Stevie
'Uggins and the utha one, Frankie
something or other, I forget e's bleedin name,
but this is the great idea: they all put 'alf a crown
in the kitty. The first matchbox that was opened up
by Mr Andretti, Peter 'is name was, they'd won.
Right, Saturday mornin', they take 'em down to Epping.
Joey 'Ooker, e's got this lovely blue pigeon,
he's got 'im in, cos you gotta get 'em inta the loft,
right, *douwn* went the ring in the matchbox,
off shoots Frankie like a bleedin' rockct
to find Stevie who's waiting at 'Oxten Markit,
to carry on the relay, you know it's like the Olympics.
Anyway, 'e dropped the bleedin' matchbox
'an it went under one of the stalls. By the time 'e found

it everybody was in! Joey 'Ooker's doin' 'is nut
and 'e's chasing Stevie for three bleedin' days
to get hold of 'im, 'an 'e's telling punters 'e was paid
by the hour to drop the bloody box!

The Bermondsey Kid

This story's about a fella they called the Bermondsey Kid
whoever 'e was. 'E was one of these street entertainers
used-ta do the markets, like Chapel Street, 'Oxten Street,
    Ridley Road,

up Kingsland Way, wherever there was a market. Well this
    particular
Saturday he decided to do a turn down on 'Oxten Street.
From the corner of Wilmer Gardens to up by Lindop, all the
    totters'

stalls was out. On the other side they were selling fourp'ny
    rabbits,
meat and gauld knows what. How they ever survived eating
    that rubbish
I don't know. The rabbits – a lot of people thought they were
    cats,

but Florrie Robinson used to de-*mand* that if she was buying
    a rabbit
it'd 'af to be an Ostend rabbit and it'd 'af to 'ave its coat on its
    back,
so it wasn't mistaken for a *cat*. Right, getting away from that

we're going to talk about how *won*derful it *was* to sit slap
    bang
on the kerb and see these boys do their stuff. So this poor
    little sod's with
these two blokes and they're going round with a black 'at.

'E's going to perform some really good act. 'E was an es-cape-
ologist.
The bloke who used to be the original was an American
fella called 'Arry 'Oudini but this bloke was The Bermondsey
    Kid

and 'e dun it all right. Not Houdini…OoDunnit! Right. The
    performance,
starts 'nd they tie 'im up like a bleedin' thruppney kipper,
put 'im in a *strait*jacket and fling some big fat chains around
    'im.

And they put 'im in this bleedin' great big bah-g. An 'e was
    gonna
get out of this lot in about five minutes 'e reckons. Well,
after ten minutes 'e's getting distressed and screaming blue
    murder,

shoutin' 'Let me out!' But the crowd, they've got the needle
by this point, but in a nice way, you know, they was all
    jocular
people, right, they 'ad to let 'im out. Well, the bloke who 'ad
    all the spiel,

'e was the one going round with the 'at an that. 'I apologise
    to the lot'f ya,
Ladies and Gentle-men,' 'e says, 'but The Kid 'e's not up to it
    this morning
and I don't think 'e 'ad any breakfast, so excuse 'im, but I
    can't give ya

an 'alfpenny back cos I don't know who *gave* me *what* money,'
'e says 'but anyway, we didn't get a lot'! So they chased 'em
through the streets, round the barrers, all the way back to
    Bermondsey!

The Nile

We used to go down the gas works
in Haggerston and the coal they used
to make the coke was a great big pile
called steam coal and as us kids
never use'ta have any swimming costumes
we used to run up this bloody great mount'n
of coke and coal, coming down lookin'
as black as the ace of spades
and diving in the water
which was mostly 'ot water
coming out of the cooling towers,
it cooled the ovens off and it was all warm.
But this particular day we was down there
on the Cut-h, we used to call it, or the Nile
as it was known, which was the Regent's Canal
from Bethnal Green to Clerkenwell.
So there was a boy name of Tommy Willis,
swam like a fish and the coal bargees
was tied up alongside and 'e's dived
awfa one of the bargees, hit the bloody rudder,
he couldn't see, the water was dirty,
he couldn't see the bloody rudder
and it hit 'is 'ead! And that was the last of 'im.
He was dead as a mackerel.
Knocked all 'is bloody brains out.

Well, my brother Bill,
'e was home on a leave from India,
'e'd bin in the ahmy since 'e was a boy
about fourteen. This was 1929,
I was 10 years old. And we was threatened
with 'oh, if you get caught
in that bloody Cut again that'd be your lot-uh!'
Well three or four days after this 'appened

we was straight down there.
Climbed over the wall over 'Aggerston Road,
came up the wall an 'e's coming along,
that's my brutha Bill, all tarted up
like a bleedin' sergeant major with 'is stick
an' 'is strut and 'e was with a coupla otha blokes
that was on leave with 'im – 'nd 'e says
'you bin in the Cut-h and I says 'no I ain't'
an' 'e says 'yes you 'ave, look at yer 'air'
he said, 'it's wet!' I said 'I 'aven't been in.'
'E says 'yes you 'ave, and if you 'ain't been in,
you're goin in now' So the three of 'em
got 'old of me and slung me off the bloody bridge
into the wat-er. If a barge 'ad bin goin' by
I coulda been bloody dead. Nice brotha 'e was!

Old Money

We're all on our way to woodwork. Charlie Collis
'e brings this little gold coin outta 'is pocket,

'e said 'e 'alf inched it outta his mutha's jug.
'E said if we changed it forrim we'd get a half

of whateva it was worth. 'Alf a crown
each we thought it was abawt ten bob.

So I goes to this bloke, a fruiterer on Southgit Road
an 'e give me the change of a pound!

Well I didn't know it was a sov'reign,
musta bin a bleedin' sov'reign,

but anyway that's what it was. I stashed
the 10 bob, 'ad two apples what me 'nd Johnny 'ad,

so 'e gave us 'alf a crown each, 'e was left
with a dollar an I 'ad fifteen bob! Well,

fifteen bob in those days was quite a lotta money.
So after school this ten bob was burnin'

a bleedin' 'ole in me pocket. 'Right! No 'ome tonight!
We're going ta the Brittania Theatre in 'Oxten Market

ta see tha pictures!' We 'ad a pocket fulla sweets,
'ad some chips when we wen' in, then we came out

'nd went to the caff again an' we 'ad fish 'n' chips,
a big wally, Tizer and more sweets.

By the time we got 'ome we musta been
as bleedin' sick as dogs. Florrie Robinson

wanted to know where we were an what
we'd bin up to, cos we 'ad this little smile on our faces.

We told 'er we fownd 'alf a crown an' we spent it.
'You greedy little sods,' she says, 'if you'da

brought that 'ome I'da given ya a tanner each
an' I coulda gone to tha' pictures.'

The next day Charlie Collis came up to us,
'e says his mutha was goin' up the school and findin'

who made 'im take the sov'reign outta the jug.
'E says 'e only got five shillings outta it,

what did 'e 'av to give us 'alf a crown each for?
'We dunno, but your mum's gonna 'ave a bleedin' job,'

we says, ''cos we spent it!' So 'e says, 'did ya only get 10 bob?'
I says 'yeah course we did. Not a penny more'.

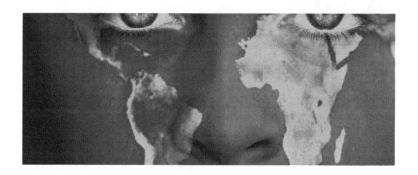

Kristiina Ehin
Estonian incantations from 'Võisiku EVAncipation'
Translated from the Estonian by Ilmar Lehtpere

Eeva (or Eva) von Bock was an Estonian peasant who married the Baltic-German nobleman Timotheus von Bock in 1817 and went to live with him at his estate in Võisiku. At the time this was an utterly astonishing occurrence in Estonia, where a very strict 'apartheid' existed between the German aristocracy, gentry, merchant and artisan classes on the one hand and the local Estonian peasantry on the other, who had until that time been serfs and therefore essentially the property of their German masters. Timotheus von Bock is the main character in the internationally renowned Estonian novelist Jaan Kross's acclaimed historical novel, *The Czar's Madman* (available in English in Anselm Hollo's excellent translation). Kristiina Ehin has said of Kross's Eeva that *'The Czar's Madman* does not in any great measure open up the world of Eeva's thoughts and feelings to us. The Eeva of *The Czar's Madman* is a proud, perfect woman who sometimes comes to haunt me with her perfection.' In her 'Võisiku EVAncipation', Kristiina Ehin gives us an altogether earthier and much more tangible Eeva – a woman steeped in the folk culture she had grown up in, finding strength and refuge, as her fellow Estonians had done for many centuries before her, in her native language and the extraordinarily rich oral tradition of folk song and incantations that this language carried, a language Estonia's German masters looked down on and hence never bothered to learn. In the following excerpt, Kristiina Ehin gives us some examples of Estonian incantations and folk song in the context of her vision of Eeva's reminiscences about putting them to use. This belief in the power of word and song permeated Estonian folk culture until very recently, indeed still continues to do so among many people, and perhaps explains why even today poets are household names in Estonian society.

Kristiina Ehin is one of the leading poets in Estonia. She has also published seven books of poetry and prose in English translation, including Popescu Prize winner *The Drums of Silence* (Oleander 2007), PBS Recommended Translation *The Scent of Your Shadow* (Arc 2010) and *The Final Going of Snow* (MPT Poets 2011). Three new translations are in preparation.

Mother taught me some words when I was a little girl. They were supposed to help if you wanted a German man to fall in love with you. When I saw my future husband for the first time, I secretly whispered this spell. It was to be spoken in one breath and after that you were to blow on your three fingers and draw them across your brow. I did that almost breathlessly with sweating, shaking hands. This is how it went:

Lord hear my voice now
I pray as one who goes astray
German man and German fellow
Fear to you, mercy to me
You smouldering wood to me
I the fire
You under the table, I on the table

You a hare, I a fox
You a bear, I a wolf
I sweeter than a tub of butter
I sweeter than a pot of honey
I sweeter than beneath a lady's apron
One land, one soil, one bone, one flesh
Jesus Christ. Amen.

But I didn't even know if I liked the man very much at first. Perhaps he was somehow too wholehearted for me, when I stop to think about it. I had been used to quite a different sort of man. My father and brothers had, ever since my childhood, indulged in irreverent banter.

In any case, I secretly recited another spell I'd learnt from some little old woman in Holstre village:

My heart hard as stone against my master
My master's heart against me soft as Mary's breasts against Jesus

And I recited:

Greetings German lord, warm stocking
I as sugar into your mouth
you as gold into my hand
You and I as secret honey in the pot.

It was a challenge to try the power of my words on a German gentleman. I knew very well that there were insurmountable barriers between Germans and Estonians.

Five there are of bloods between us
Six there are of dried up rivers
Seven springs of standing water
Eight the seas all full of fishes
Nine there are of Mother Rivers
Ten of earthen walls between us.

But we managed to slip over them. Whether it was with or without witch's spells. It is difficult to be the wife of a man who is caught up in some ordeal. For even the best man tends to pour out his anger against the world upon his wife. But I was unyielding. And I had my words. When my husband called me to once again give me a dressing-down over some trivial matter, I remembered the words that had arisen from bad blood against the Germans where I grew up. My grandfather used to say that if you want to placate the anger of the lord of the manor, you have to master the following skill. On stepping into the lord's room, left foot first, and looking straight at the lord, you have to say these words within yourself:

The wolf comes before the fog
Lambskin hat upon his head
My mind thinks about him
His mind thinks about me
I kiss the the sole of his foot
He kisses the sole of my foot
Then we will be brethren

And in my thoughts I also said:

Blue pig and red piglet
Crawl into the bushes
Your switches are yet to be cut

In this way I've been 'a wolf before the fog with a lambskin hat upon my head' all my life. I look so mild and modest that no one suspects that by night I become a wolf. My German and French are so flawless that no one would guess that I think in the language of folk song and recite spells at every step. The village people in Võisiku secretly call me the whore of the lords, the nobility half-openly call me peasant wench. I just hum to myself 'One land, one soil, one bone, one flesh . . .' I look them in the eye and in my thoughts I say, 'We are brethren.'

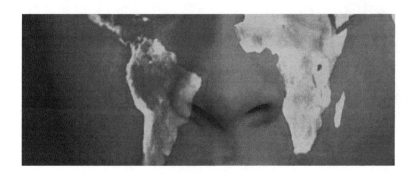

Philip Gross
Three sections from 'Something Like The Sea'

One day you woke to find that you'd lost barley.
Oats. Wheat. Tried each of your five languages
and nothing answered to its name.

You stared through a sixty-year gap in the trees,
past the farmhouse, out into the fields
(all-angled, small, pre-Soviet)

of wordlessness. What you were seeing there
wasn't nothing. *This one . . .* You tensed
your fingers, upwards. *And this . . .*

Your fingers tremble-dangled. 'Oats?' *Yes!*
Yes. And that itching-and-scratching
down the back of your neck:

threshed husks in the shade of the barn. Later
hordeum and *triticum* came to you, then
some English, some Estonian.

But you'd been back there, in the gone place,
absolutely, with each *Ding an sich.*
You'd been it, and no words between.

*

I've lost you, way back,

several crumbling sentences ago.
A dead end . . . —*eeee*—
one long wince of a vowel.
You've paused,

as at a locked gate
you might once have climbed.
Ich . . . habe . . . nicht . . . you've said, then
S-, or *sch-*, or *z-?* And ends in *–l* . . .

Seele? Soul? I trace
the definition. No, *Ziel?* Purpose?
Yes, you're nodding: *end;*
objective; point . . . And so

much hangs on who's defining:
some sage wrestling manhood from the hard
thin Alp-air of abstractions . . . or
some bully with a few insignia

and the right to tell
this shamble of Ostlanders (not Aryan
but not Slav-subhuman) what purpose
they serve. The word looks on,

beyond translation. *Ziel (neuter):*
purpose;
          target;
                   finish;
                            destination;
home.

*

On a calm day the gaps, the audible
ellipses, become *la-la-la-la-la*—

the way that most tongues sing along
when we don't have the words.

I know this in my scant Estonian: that *laul,*
is song. John, stay in those days,

not the flurries of hard consonants, the *ka-*,
the *ga-*. that come with finger-stabbing

and a hunted look. *Lully, lulla . . .* I wish you
the Coventry Carol, comfort on the edge

of any language, its *lully, lulla, lullay*

**The poems printed here are from a new collection *Deep Field*,
to be published by Bloodaxe in November 2011.**

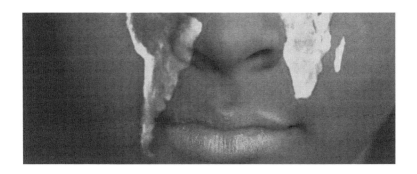

Iain Galbraith
'God Tamangur'

Responding to a commission, not to translate – at least not in any conventional inter-lingual sense – Peider Lansel's Rheatian 'l'homme armé' itself, but to write a poem taking its inspiration from his 'Tamangur', I set about learning some Romansh. I suppose I thought that by learning the rudiments of the language I would be able to take part in basic conversation at a festival of poetry and music to which I had been invited; perhaps also to show some respect to the Romansh writers, who would, when I met them, or so I imagined, shame me with their fluency in German, French and Italian. However, my initial embarrassment at the presumption of jump-starting a poem from work in a rare tongue that I did not understand rapidly developed into a fascination with the language itself. I read histories of Romansh – including Joseph Planta's 'Account of the Romansh Language' (1775) in his scholarly letter to Sir John Pringle and the Royal Society – and I studied its grammar and lexicon, participating in online language courses and soliciting what help I could from the experts. Some knowledge of Latin and early French must have hastened my progress, for it was not long before I was able to gain an impression – with the help of dictionaries like the *Pledari grond* or *My Pledari* – of the scope and texture of Peider Lansel's 'Tamangur'. It does not do to devour a language too quickly,

however, and since those giddy, yet pleasurably focused days, I
have forgotten almost everything that I learned. At the time,
my studies revealed to me that Lansel had included words from
different dialects in his poem, whose composition in 1923 had
long preceded the recent establishment of any unified, standard
Romansh. To translate the poem into a standard language, as
did two German versions that I had compared with the original,
was to lose much of the poem's massy hybridity. Perhaps it was
the attraction of this dilemma, or perhaps it was the mirror
the poem inadvertently held up to the fate of the Caledonian
pine forest, that sent me translating, as closely as possible,
Lansel's 'Tamangur' – bringing its orderly rhymes to bear on
the intoxicating impurities of a kind of 'Inglis' lexical synthesis.
The poem compares the plight of a particular forest at one end
of the Val S-Charl, in Swiss Engadine, to that of the Romansh
language. The God Tamangur is the highest Cembro Pine Forest
in Europe and is linked to a potent myth. For it is said that the
Romansh language will survive only for as long as the forest itself
continues to exist. 'God' is the Romansh word for forest, and it
was this that suggested the title of my own poem, 'The Portage
of the God'. At one level this poem dramatizes the events of the
third stanza of Peider Lansel's work – 'Came foolish folk upon
the scene / cutting shank and shelter branch' – but 'The Portage
of the God' is also a poem about translation, or rather, about the
quandary of being translated. At yet another level, 'The Portage
of the God' can be read without any reference at all to the 'God
Tamangur' or the danger of its 'owersettin' (a Scots word that can
mean overturning or overpowering, and also translation).

Peider Lansel (1863–1943)

Tamangur

Aintasom S-charl (ingio sun rafüdats
tuots oters gods) sün spuonda vers daman,
schi varsaquants veidrischems dschembers stan
da vegldüm i strasoras s-charplinats.
Tröp sco l'ingual nu's chatta plü ninglur,
ultim avanz d'ün god, dit: «Tamangur.»

Da plü bodun quel sgüra cuvernet
costas e spis cha bluots uossa vezain;
millieras d'ans passettan i scumbain
ch'ardênn sajettas e cha naiv terret,
ha tantüna la vita gnü vendschur
i verdagià trasoura Tamangur.

Mo cur umbras l'uman gnit be sdrüand
sainza ningün pissêr sün il davo,
schi lavinas e boudas s'fettan pro.
L'ajer dvantet vi'e plü crü, fintant
nu madürênn plü'ls bös-chs las puschas lur
i daspö quai al main jet Tamangur.

As dostand fin l'ultim, in davo man
ils dschembers ün ad ün, sco schlass sudats
chi sül champ da battaglia sun crodats,
per terra vi'smarscheschan plan a plan. –
Id ajüd chi nu vain bainbod – Dalur! –
svanirà fina'l nom da Tamangur.

Al veider god, chi pac a pac gnit sdrüt
sumeglia zuond eir nos linguach prüvà,
chi dal vast territori d'üna jà
in usché strets cunfins uoss'es ardüt.
Scha'ls Rumanschs nu fan tuots il dovair lur,
jaraj'a man cun el, sco Tamangur.

Co invlüdessans, ch'el da seculs nan
savet noss vegls da redscher i guidar?
Jerta ch'adüna tgnettan adachar,
varguogna bain! sch'la dessans our da man.
Tgnain vi dal nos, sco'ls oters vi dal lur
e'ns algordain la fin da Tamangur.

Be nö'dar loc! – Ningün nu podrà tour
a la schlatta rumanscha 'l dret plü ferm,
chi'd es quel: da mantgnair dadaint seis term
uoss'id adüna, seis linguach dal cour –
Rumantschs dat pro! – spendrai tras voss'amur
nos linguach da la mort da Tamangur.

Peider Lansel

Tamangur

High in Scarl Glen behind
the other forests stands a group
of stone pines on the eastern slope
riven by age & harried by wind
a trip o trees o makless valour
remenant cleped Tamangur.

Time was that saw it grow
on shins & ridges bare today
millennia went with clash & fray
of lightning fire & hurling snow
but life sae thrawn will aye endure
& ayeweys green grew Tamangur.

Came foolish folk upon the scene
cutting shank & shelter-branch
sowing landslide & avalanche
& when the air turned sore & keen
the caller cones could na mature
& ayeweys less grew Tamangur.

Till bitter end it would not yield
but one by one the pine-trees fell
the pretty soldiers slain in battle
have since lain rotting in the field
faut o succour soon will smoor
the vera nem o Tamangur.

An ancient forest's gradual ruin
how like our mother tongue's decline
what overclad a great domain
is now confined to strait terrain
gin Rheatians willna fin a cure
our leid shall fail lik Tamangur.

Who will forget that from the first
it led our kin & lit their heart
they held it in such high regard
what shame indeed if it be lost
as ithers thairs ours let us traisure
& mind the end o Tamangur.

But never swither none can sever
us from ancient Romansh right
which is within our bounds to fight
to keep a cherished tongue forever
Rheatians sauf yer leid-amour
evite the deid o Tamangur.

Translated from the Romansh by Iain Galbraith

Iain Galbraith

The Portage of the God

They came out of the heavens,
whence those hackers of shoulder and shin
took a sighting of all that I was.
They came in the evening before the sun
had retired to the back of the crags.
They fed and I was overset,
without witness carried to a country
where I must die as I lived.

I do not speak as if I were home.
I do not speak as if I were lying,
dead or dying on these paper-thin slopes.
They keep me in holy places.
They talk to me daily.
In silence I answer the question
they cannot cease to ask.

We have seen you, so they say,
dividing and dividing again
our thrones, our armies, all our holy orders.
We have watched your green-throated birds
hop through the spirals of our substance.
Dendrites flood with your sap,
our families descend through your limbs.
In our bareness of mountains and waves
spate-water follows your behest,
happy to desert its offspring
on the steep flanks of the fells.

We have given you a past.
In return you have filled our archives,
inventing names for the jade-metalled roads
which criss-cross our children's wrists.
Your ring-works tell our story.
We are the key
to the shapes you make,
the reason your fingers draw cracks in the sky.

This they say to me,
an elegy on the face of the orphaned earth.
They say it with my words.

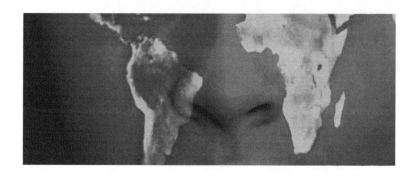

Seán Ó Ríordáin
Two poems
Translated from the Irish by Gerry Byrne

Seán Ó Ríordáin (1916–1977) was born in Baile Mhúirne, County
Cork, with English as his first language and he acquired Irish,
spoken by his father and other members of the family, as he grew
up. While Ó Ríordáin wrote in Irish, it appears that he always
struggled with a sense of loss and alienation from Irish language
and culture, in part a consequence of his upbringing bilingually,
but also because he was influenced by European literature and
culture. Ó Ríordáin published four volumes of poetry, *Eireaball
Spideoige* (A Robin's Tail, 1952), *Brosna* (A Handful of Twigs,
1964), *Lìnte Liombó* (Lines from Limbo) and the posthumous *Tar
Éis Mo Bháis* (After My Death).

Ó Ríordáin believed that poetry should derive from a moment
of revelation – *'geit'* meaning 'a startling' – in which sudden
contact with the essential nature of a thing or a living creature
outside of the self is made through the power of imagination. A
moment of revelation that potentially changes one's perspective
simultaneously on the self and the other, allowing for contact
across the tribal divides.

Altering

'C'mere,' says Turnbull, 'so that you see the sorrow
In this horse's eyes,
If you had hooves as big as those under you there'd be sorrow
In your eyes, same as his.'

And it was clear that he understood so, so well the sorrow
In the horse's eyes
And he imagined so intensely in the end
He dove into the mind of the horse.

I looked at the horse so that I too might see the sorrow
Standing there in his eyes.
I saw, from the head of the horse, looking right back at me
The eyes of Turnbull.

I looked at Turnbull, once, and then again
And I saw in his sloping cheeks
Those great, great eyes, dumb with sorrow –
The eyes of the horse.

The Cat

What! Leave the cat outside
        Alone in the blind-night,
And the sky too high as a house?
        I would not do such a thing.

Two eyes burning like cigarettes
        Far off in the deep of night –
Terror in a kitten's heart:
        I would not do such a thing.

Combed whiskers trembling
        Claws ready to fight,
Break a kitten's trust?
        I would not do such a thing.

For I drank of the cat's thoughts
        And studied the cat closely
The thoughts pouring in through my eye
        And we grew as one.

I was made half-cat
        And likewise the cat became human.
Split our cohabitation?
        I would not do such a thing.

The ancient hatred cats hold
        For the human race itself
In those eyes of his I sensed –
        That I would always be in pain.

Charles Cantalupo
Translating African-Language Poetry:
Is There Enough?

When I was in Asmara, Eritrea, last summer, I was asked a
lot about my new book, *War and Peace in Contemporary Eritrean
Poetry*, published by Mkuki na Nyota Publishers in Dar es
Salaam in 2009. The book was rejected by just about every
publisher in the United States and England who publish titles
in African literature, as well as by a clutch of publishers who I
thought should be publishing on African literature, and nearly
all stated the same reason in their rejection letters: the topic
was too narrow. In short, there really wasn't enough – subject
matter or readership – to warrant such a book. Such an editorial
judgment went against my own thinking, which I stated in the
first sentence of the book's Foreword: that to discuss the entire
contemporary poetry of most if not all countries requires more
than a book, and Eritrea is no exception. My book covers selected
poems by Eritrean poets of roughly the last three decades and
who write in three of Eritrea's nine languages.

In my view the African-language poetry of nearly every country
of Africa, or of most African languages – be they national or
transnational or regional – warrants such a book-length study
as mine of contemporary Eritrean poetry in Tigrinya, Tigre and
Arabic. And not just Africa. My colleague at Penn State, Michael

Naydan, translates and publishes books of Ukrainian poetry and fiction. His multiform efforts have created a kind of critical mass that establishes Ukrainian literature in the annals of world literature. Moreover, through translation he has majoritized a previously minoritized literature: minoritized, I should add, by a political history of brutal proportions and intensity. Of the 1500 writers Stalin had executed in the 1930s, at least half were Ukrainian. A plethora of literary talent, they were, in Naydan's term, 'an Executed Renaissance' (see *MPT* 3/14 and 15). In African-language literature, we are only just beginning to uncover any number of examples of 'an Executed Renaissance' of writers or poets and storytellers. And we struggle to prevent such executions from continuing.

But imagine my surprise, again in Asmara last summer and being interviewed about the book for state-run media, when I was asked, 'Do you really feel there is enough material in the domain of Eritrean literature to begin producing literary "criticism" on the subject?'

I date the beginning of Eritrean literature to a stele in the southern part of the country, a region famous for its poets, near a small place called Belew Kelew, meaning 'two brothers'. The stele is three to four thousand years old. A lot of literature, including orature or oral literature, has come between then and now. Not that we know it all, or even much of it. Fiction, nonfiction, poetry, drama, journalism – Eritrean literature has it all. There is plenty. I say this with total confidence, even though I only know the literature, for the most part, through translation. Thus far we are only scratching the surface (the same can be said for archaeology in Eritrea). Where there is language there is poetry; there is literature. And Eritrea has nine languages, which means nine literatures, at least. The opportunities for writers and scholars in Eritrean languages and literatures are innumerable. To take one outstanding recent example: the national Eritrean publisher, Hdri, has put out a new anthology of Tigre language stories, poetry, tales, curses, blessings, and more. The book is monumental, and begs for literary-critical and scholarly attention.

Still, this question – is there enough? – raises an important issue. Where does the doubt come from that there might not be enough Eritrean literature, or even that it might not suit the usual purposes of literary study and criticism? I also ran into doubt when I first had the idea of translating contemporary Eritrean poetry.

In 1998 when I first heard Eritrean poetry at the Expo festival, I was amazed and full of admiration for what I heard. My response also included a desire to try to translate it, a not unusual, even a predictable, feeling for a poet and a professor to have.

Nevertheless, when I asked my friend, an Eritrean / American publisher, whether he would be interested in a book of such translations, he answered, 'I would love to do it, but Tigrinya poetry is tough if not impossible to translate. All the levels of meanings and the wide range of linguistic references might not carry over, but you could try. Ask the poet himself.'

Which was what I did, but not without wondering why translating Tigrinya might be considered impossible, when nearly every other language in the world – or at least every language that I had ever heard of – allowed for at least some kind of translation. Was Tigrinya different? Was that why there were virtually no translations, except for some early 20th-century renderings in Italian?

A few days later, when I met the poet and asked him, 'Has anyone ever translated one of your poems in Tigrinya', he replied matter of factly, 'No. It would be too difficult. Tigrinya has too much to get across.' Remembering that my publisher friend had been similarly discouraging, either I didn't care or didn't believe that Tigrinya was so unique among languages that it couldn't be translated. 'Still, I'd like to try,' I answered.

Twelve years later, last summer I returned to Eritrea for its judgment on the results: four books, a documentary, and some translations of Eritrean oral poetry, too. The record was far from perfect, but I never thought it could be. As I was fairly warned from the beginning, poetry in Tigrinya, like poetry in Eritrea's other languages that I have translated, does have 'levels of meanings and [a] wide range of linguistic references . . . [that do] not carry over'. The poems are 'too difficult' and do have 'too much to get across'. Still, I don't know of any great poems in English or any language for which the same might not be said: the Sundiata epic, Homer, Dante, Gilgamesh, all the poetry in the Hebrew and Greek Bible, the Scriptures in Ge'ez, the great Modernist poems of the 20th century. The list is endless. As is written in Ecclesiastes (12:12), 'of making many books there is no end.'

But again, let me ask: is there enough? If one looks around, there doesn't seem to be. Yet if there is, and we don't see it, there must be a failure of translating African-language literature: a failure that I find in particular in translating African-language poetry.

Discretion is the better part of valour, and I will not name names, but every single, major international poetry journal or website – even of translated literature – is complicit in this failure since their publishing African-language poetry or literature in general is minimal or non-existent. Every major anthology of African literature is similarly complicit and, even when they do include African-language work, the translation and the accompanying scholarship are usually abysmal.

The failure of translating African language poetry derives first from a failure to recognize the primacy of African languages for African poetry. African literature exists primarily in African languages, which require translation; yet ironically, African literature that is translated amounts to even less than what exists in colonial languages, which is also slight in comparison with the literature in African languages. Moreover, among nearly all readers of African poetry and African literature in general, there is a failure to acknowledge that it is primarily a body of work that requires translation.

But why has so little African-language poetry, from the past and/or contemporary – in all of its vast and varied richness – been translated, and why has what has been translated had such a negligible effect on readers worldwide? For the most part, I can no longer attribute such a wild imbalance to bad or ulterior motives. It can and has been explained – accurately, in my view – according to well-known political formulae about the destructive nature of colonialism and neo-colonialism; but such remedial efforts have not seemed to help a lot in resolving the matter either, whatever the start that has been made.

So what's the problem? More specifically, I mean why aren't more editors and publishers, readers and writers clamouring for more African-language translation, and supporting it themselves with their own actions? What's stopping them?

In addition to the lack of work that is published and, in what is published, the generally low level of literary-critical value and scholarly discussion, here are two more possible answers to the question.

1. **An underdeveloped poetics for African-language poetry translation.** While many African writers who work in African languages contend that poems in these languages have elaborate sound and metric patterns, their translations almost invariably appear in free verse, without availing themselves of elaborate sound and metric patterns in the target language – English, for instance – that might make the poems more substantial and enjoyable to the target audience. Take the example of Mazisi Kunene, 20th-century Zulu's greatest poet and its greatest translator. While he can write page after page about Zulu poetics, when he turns to the poetics of his translations into English he can only offer that he relies on 'an internal rhythm'.

2. **The promotion of the work's political or anthropological value at the expense of its literary value.** I think the failure of translating African-language poetry is due to an over-emphasis on anthropological and folkloric values of authenticity – both in sound and sense – and on issues of racial and ethnic identity considered to be inseparable from social and political advocacy for personal and/or national liberation. The powerful and inspiring liberation narratives of writers like Ngugi wa Thiong'o, Kofi Awoonor and Kofi Anyidoho, and Mazisi Kunene

notwithstanding, they bear a burden of concerns that great literature need not necessarily have, although nearly all great African literature, frankly, has been stereotyped with this. I would argue that translators of African-language poetry now must find a way for their poetics to triumph over the vitriol of politics as African poetry joins global forces in search of connection. Paeans to Mother Africa, pan-African aspirations that seem further from actually happening than ever before, African essentialism and exceptionalism, cultural stereotypes that presuppose that African languages and literatures are necessarily best understood by Africans and/or the African diaspora, and praising Africa at the expense of Europe or the west by more or less simply reversing the trope of 'dark continent', generally make bad poetry. The radical displacement of African languages historically by colonial languages and presently by global languages has precipitated the relative absence and impotence of African languages and their poetry – both themselves and in translation – in the world of international letters, but so has the relatively poor quantity and quality of translations of African-language poetry, a widespread misunderstanding among translators of critical issues and goals of literary translation, and a similar misunderstanding of the critical standards of quality literary journals and the means of their cultural production.

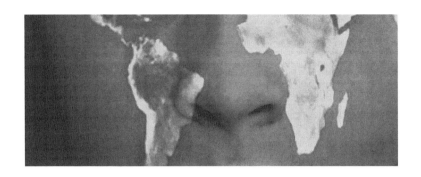

Víctor Terán
Five poems
Translated from the Zapotec by David Shook

Víctor Terán is the most personal poet of the Zapotec Isthmus of Oaxaca, Mexico. He was born in Juchitán de Zaragoza in 1958. His work has been published extensively in magazines and anthologies throughout Mexico and the world. A three-time recipient of the National Fellowship for Writers of Indigenous Languages, his most recent book is *The Spines of Love*. Terán is an active promoter of contemporary Zapotec literature. Recent translations of his poems by David Shook have appeared in *Agenda*, *Hayden's Ferry Review*, *Oxford Magazine*, *Poetry*, *World Literature Today*, and elsewhere, and have been nominated for a Pushcart. A chapbook is available from the Poetry Translation Centre.

The following poems are from his book of Zapotec-language children's poetry.

Bendabuaa

Ziuula' guicharuaa
riguude ne rigaa
ninou' tindaa beeu laa
ne ra nisado' rigaa.

The Shrimp

Has two long beards,
bends & lengthens.
He's a slice of the moon
fished for in the sea.

Chisa

Cadi lexu laa,
huaga laaca co'.
Tindaa dxiibi la?
rilui', huaxa co'.

The Squirrel

It's not a rabbit
or a rat.
A slice of fear?
It looks like it, but nope.

Nagande

Necape' napa' bidxichi
guidibo'co qui nizie',
nuuyapia' guiza' nidxiichi,
xine, pa gande batanee.

The Centipede

Even if I had money
I wouldn't buy him shoes.
I'm sure he'll be mad,
but why, if he has so many
      feet?

Gubidxa

Rului' ti suquii,
suquii naze gui
ra rugaagui Diuxi
ni gue', go ne goxhi.

The Sun

It looks like an oven,
a lit oven,
where God cooks
all his food.

Berendxinga

Chuppa guicharuaa
ne lu ca xhoopa' na'
zuuyu' berendxinga
cayuunda' deche dxia.

Nadiine ruunda'
na ti bichube,
bicabi ti bandaa:
lii bigani dxe.

Naguude guicharuaa
ne cadi huadxi laa,
xisi lade xhiaa
ridxi que rira.

The Cricket

Two antennas like beards
& high on his six feet
you'll see the cricket sing
over the stovetop.

He sings really bad,
says the snail.
The termite responds:
shut up, you fool!

His antennas bend
& he's almost without
    importance
but between his wings
his song never ends.

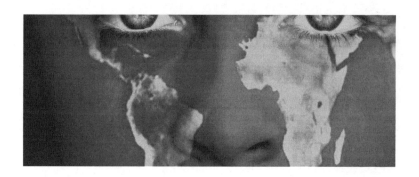

Max Rouquette
Three poems
Translated from the Occitan by
Teleri Williams

Max Rouquette (1908-2005) was born in Argelliers in the
Hérault *département* of the Languedoc. During his childhood
the first language of the inhabitants of rural villages such as his
would have been Occitan, and he chose to write first in Occitan,
although this meant he was relatively unrecognised in France.
Only later did he translate his work into French. As he began to
publish his poetry he became interested in cultural groups such
as Le Nouveau Languedoc and made contact with Catalan and
Occitan intellectuals. In 1945 he helped to found the Institute of
Occitan Studies and became a passionate defender and promoter
of Occitan language and culture .

His long life and writing career resulted in a large body of
work, from his early poetry collections *Sòmis dau matin* (Morning
Dreams, 1937) and *Sòmis de la nuòch* (Night Dreams, 1942) to the
poems of his old age in *D'aicí mil ans de lutz* (A thousand light
years from here, 1995). His dramatic and prose pieces include
his best-known work *Verd Paradís* (Green Paradise, 1961 and
1974). The latter is an exploration in poetic prose of the nature,

culture and folk traditions of the village and the *garrigue* (the wild vegetation on the Mediterranean hills) where Rouquette grew up. Rouquette is the rememberer and reviver of a way of life which has been threatened with extinction over the century since his birth.

The borders of Occitania are vague – its area covers much of southern France and Occitan is spoken from the valleys of the Italian Alps to the Pyrenees where the Val d'Aran in Catalunya is the only place where it is an official language. But for its people the land, its rocks, earth, vegetation and the food it produces, are essential to their identity. Rouquette's work paints a picture of loss: 'La lenga s'es perduda' (The language is lost) laments the forgotten names for the wild herbs of the *garrigue*, 'la frigola, lo reponchon e lo renebre' (thyme, rampion and sorrel). At the same time his work preserves those names and their environment, a place where the language shimmers in fragile reflections of spring water that is 'fosca de sos secrèts lontans' ('dark with its distant secrets' – in 'Lo Silenci', The Silence).

Although deeply rooted in this environment, Rouquette did not confine his thinking to the world of a small village. While celebrating his native culture and environment, he also looked outwards to other countries, other languages, with a sense of common humanity. In 'L'argela' (Clay) he begins with the quite similar words in Occitan and Spanish for this geological substance and then moves out to other poets in South America and Spain, and eventually to our common mortality and humanity's insignificance in the universe.

Renebre

Renebre, dins ton dire, las aradas,
la talh dubèrt que lusís au solelh.
Renebre, un dire tot dins sa paraula:
renebre, dins son agre e dins son libre, un pòble.
Un pòble dins sa patz, luònhta la guèrra,
luònh, l'espada, lo fuòc, lo raubatòri.
Urós lo pòble aquel que sa vertut
es de veire lusir per sa claror las èrbas
quand las fai rire lo solelh.
Urós lo pòble dau renebre e de la ceba
e dau fiu d'òli sus lo pan,
ont s'enauça lo pan a la claror divenca.
Urós lo pòble de l'alhada e de l'anchòia.
E dau rasim de lutz dins la claror dels dets.
La patz s'estira en sa paraula,
l'aculhença au còr de sas mans,
e lusís son agach, claror frairala.
S'apila a la vertat de tota causa,
sa vertat, de la tèrra i ven,
e s'es simple de còr es que sa vida
es teissuda coma l'estòfa de las èrbas.
Renebre, tèrra-grèpia et tu, lachuscla,
e l'òli de l'oliu, lo vinagre dau vin,
lo pan dau blat, lo legum de la tèrra,
aquí, paraulas de vertat.

E lo vent fèr de las combas fonsudas.

Renebre – Fiddle Dock

Renebre, in the saying of your name, the ploughing,
the open furrow that shines in the sun.
Renebre, a whole world in its name:
renebre, a people at home and free.
A people in peace, far from war,
far from the sword, the fire, from exile.
Happy, the people whose nature
is to see the light in the grasses
when the sun makes them laugh.
Happy, the people of the fiddle dock and the onion,
and the stream of oil on their bread
that raises it to divine light.
Happy, the people of garlic soup and anchovies.
And of grapes of light between their fingers.
Peace fills their speech,
the welcome in their open hands,
and its expression shines with clear friendship.
They draw on the truth of everything,
their truth that came to them from the earth,
and if they are simple in their hearts and in their life,
their fabric is like the flesh of grass.
Renebre, *tèrra-grèpia* and you, *lachuscla*,
oil from olives, vinegar from wine,
bread from wheat, food plants from the earth,
these are the true words.

And the wild wind from the deep valleys.

Translator's Note: In his own French version of this poem Max
Rouquette translates *renebre* as *sanguisorbe* (Great Burnet in English)
but it seems more likely that he meant a variety of wild sorrel known
in French as *patience violon* and in English as the Fiddle Dock. I like the
unintended pun on *langue d'oc* involved in the English name.
tèrra-grèpia: scorzonera
lachuscla: sow-thistle

A thousand light years from here
(D'aquí mil ans de lutz)

Although it wasn't the voice that whispered to me,
    murmuring on the moss,
its breath so soft in the shadows of the old garden,
where the birds and the wind played flutes
at the hour when the kiss of the sun softened.
And although it wasn't the horizon of palms,
horizon of the islands under the wind.
It wasn't the palm of a hand on the grey plaster of the walls,
nor the mulberry tree shading, hiding the cold water of the
    spring;
a dark passing that entered my soul
and I don't recognise the words that well up from it
and neither do I know the dreams it tells me.
So many nights in the dark world,
even more than a thousand light years from here.
And I hear this faceless voice in the darkness where it hides,
curious like a child told stories
on winter nights, windy and black as soot,
and who shivers and hugs his knees,
but who, should he die, would want only
that the words rising from the abyss be silenced
where time comes to put away its sickles
under the vaults of spiders' webs.

The river (Lo flume)

Look at the river sliding slowly
    down from the timeless mountains.
The angels have folded their huge wings
    dazzling as snow.
Silent angels, fingers to their lips,
    in a great silence like night.
In a silence without echo
    where all words are lost.

Look at the river sliding slowly.
    It takes no notice of you.
It passes and takes the sun with it.
    And the overhanging trees
are left with only the image.
    Their shadows drown in the deep
water that cradles the grasses.

    Don't lean over the surface of the river
your face yearning to draw
    from the whirlpools some face
some memory from on high.

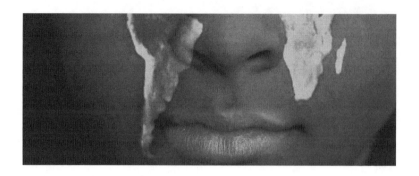

Claude Vigée
From *Black Nettles Blaze in the Wind*
Translated from the Alsatian by
Delphine Grass

This translation is an extract from Claude Vigée's long Alsatian requiem *Schwàrzi Sengessle Flàckere ém Wénd* (Black Nettles Blaze in the Wind), written in 1982 in Israël. During the Second World War, Claude Vigée was forced into exile from his hometown of Bischwiller and moved to the United States, where he became a professor of French literature. He once described himself as a 'Jew and an Alsatian, thus doubly Alsatian and doubly Jewish'. As well as a prolific poet who has won the Prix Goncourt de la Poésie Française in 2008, he is also an essayist and a translator.

The poem from which this extract is taken is an ode to the family, childhood friends and country he was forced to leave behind, as well as a tribute to his native dialect, which many children were forbidden to speak in schools when French became once more the official language. For many Alsatians, the famous quotation attributed to Max Weinreich: 'A language is a dialect with an army and navy' has had to be taken literally more than once. Yet the different registers of this poem, which range from the elegiac to the comical and grotesque, could be read as a testimony to the idiomatic and colloquial forms present in *all* languages.

Being a mere 'silent' practitioner of Alsatian (I understand much of it but I do not speak it), I would like to thank my mother and aunt for helping me with this translation.

Weil's unverhofft eruffgschosse n'ésch
un dànn au wédder glisch
zeruckgschluckt word,
dess ewisch ungschproche kénderword,
wurum schtehm'r àlli so dumm un so krumm
wie bettler mét lèeri händ
einfäldi un hélfloos doo?

Unser läwe làng
hémmrs uff urlaub gschikt:
desshàlb sémmr àlmäli au métverschickt,
mr sähn émmer e béssel vergälschdert üss
un schîne hàlwer schtumm.
Vun jeh-hèr gerbroche
schtockt unsri haiseri schtémm:
mièr àngeboreni zwàngs-schproochkréppel,
mr sénn ewe verwurixt
ém ajene gsàng!

Wàss hets schun genutzt, déss schelde n'un schbotte?
wàss blît uns ützer éwrisch, nooch alli unsre schànd?
Gràd noch e loch ém sàck
vum verfetzte fààssenààchtsgewànd.
Nur eins gelingt uns armi doddel:
Schtéll bràf sénn, un barrière.
Déss ésch dr lohn vum eschte hosseloddel.
'Numme ne-béssel geduld',
henn frihr unsri herre-lehrer àls
uns jungi hitzkepf zügeroode.
'Binde-néisch nur nit selwer de schtràng um de hàls.

s'hett sisch schun mànischer föjel
sinn brobbers fedderenescht verschésse:
àlso verschteckle n'ièhr gànz gerésse
éiri schàrefi gràlle under d'sàmmet-pfoode,
genau wie dr madam Méller ièhre moller!
Schunsch word éisch durisch éiri ajeni schuld
ém läwe nemool ebbs viel schlémmeres bàssière:
dr mensch weiss ewe nie, wàss'em kànn zügeroode . . .'
Un so nawelt sisch jeder selbscht d'kett àn de koller.

Since it erupted in our windpipes
as quickly as it had vanished
gulped down at the bottom of our wells –
the forever silenced language of childhood –
Why do we stand there like helpless beggars,
all dazed and crooked
bare hands extending?

All this life we dismissed it
on the grounds of sickness:
though slowly stifling ourselves
as we stood away from it.
Always, this foolish air of panic,
of being struck half-dumb.
Our hoarse voices, broken long ago
suddenly stopped:
already, on our school bench,
in the thrall of the forceps of language
we felt like tongue-cripples
tangled up in our songs!
What would be the point
of anger or scorn?
What do we have left
after all this hurt?

A bottomless tear
in the empty pockets
of our ragged and tattered
carnival costumes.
The only trick that seemed to work for us:
be good now, and do as they say –
that's the lot of true poor wretches.
'Patience, patience',
advised the professors
to us hotheads,
'Do not bend the rope too quickly around your necks:
for many a bird before has shat on its own nest.
Be clever, like Mrs Méller's cat,
keep your claws hidden
in a velvet glove,
or may you endure the guilt
of having cursed yourselves
with the plagues and havocs of the entire world:
God knows what will happen then!'
– and so we single-handedly
clinched the nail
that clung to our shackles.

Pier Paolo Pasolini
Three poems
Translated from the Friulian by Marina
Della Putta Johnston and Taije Silverman

Pier Paolo Pasolini originally wrote these poems during the 1940s, using the Friulian dialect of his mother's hometown, Casarsa della Delizia, to describe life in the Northern Italian region where he spent childhood summers and later lived during World War II. It was in Casarsa that Pasolini discovered his homosexuality, embraced communism but was expelled from the Communist party, and experienced his younger brother's death at the hands of an extremist faction of fellow communists. These early poems reflect both the poet's devotion to the verdant landscape and peasant culture of his ancestral home and his realization that he didn't belong there. He collected them as his first major book, *La meglio gioventù* (The Finest Youth) in 1954.

Pasolini rewrote the poems decades later during the 'Years of Lead' when Italy suffered massive acts of political terrorism. By then, he had become a leading film director in Rome; Casarsa was a lost paradise, and these new versions betray Pasolini's distance from it. He published both forms together as *La nuova gioventù* (The New Youth) in 1975, citing as the book's motivation his 'mania for repetition' and 'terror at never being able to say the definitive last word.' This mania manifests itself in the poet's word choice, structures, and overlapping themes, with the repeated motifs of his brother's death, his mother's devastation, and his own inability (often present through the image of Narcissus as the mutable yet trapped self) to go back in time.

Only these first and last of Pasolini's seven poetry collections were in dialect. The others employ the traditional and experimental verse of standard Italian, and they built his reputation as a political poet. His Friulian poems are quite different – lyrical, mysterious, and equally rooted in landscape and myth, their thick, truncated sound seems unrelated to the clearer, rounder melody of Italian. When Pasolini taught elementary school in Friuli during the 1940s, students would have been more comfortable speaking Friulian than Italian despite the Fascist government's attempt to suppress it. One of the few of Italy's numerous dialects recognized as an official language, Friulian is still widely spoken and now carefully protected.

<table>
<tr><td>

Dedication (first version)

Water fountain in my small town.
There's no fresher water
than the water in my town.
Fountain of rustic love.

</td><td>

Dedica – *La meglio gioventú* (1941–53)

Fontana di aga dal me país,
A no è aga pí fres-cia che tal me país.
Fontana di rustic amòur.

</td></tr>
<tr><td>

Dedication (second version)

Water fountain in a foreign town.
There's no older water
than the water in that town.
Fountain of no one's love.

</td><td>

Dedica – *Seconda forma de 'La meglio gioventú'* (1974)

Fontana di aga di un país no me.
A no è aga pí vecia che ta chel país.
Fontana di amòur par nissún.

</td></tr>
</table>

The Dead Boy (first version)

Luminous dusk, gully filling
with water, a woman with child
weaves her way through a field.

Narcissus, I remember you.
You were the colour of dusk
when death bells toll.

The Dead Boy (second version)

Luminous dusk and the gully's
gone dry, the shade of a woman
weaves its way through a field.

Though I haven't returned and don't dream of you,
Narcissus, I still know you were the hue
of dusk when the bells tolled May.

Il nini muàrt — *La meglio gioventú* (1941–53)

Sera imbarlumida, tal fossàl
a cres l'aga, na fèmina plena
a ciamina pal ciamp.

Jo ti recuardi, Narcís, ti vèvis il colòur
da la sera, quand li ciampanis
a súnin di muàrt.

Il nini muàrt — *Seconda forma de 'La meglio gioventú'* (1974)

Sera imbarlumida, il fossàl
al è sec, l'ombrena di 'na fèmina plena
a ciamina pa'l ciamp.

Sensa tornà nè insumiati, Narcís, i sai
enciamò ch'i ti vevis il colòur da la sera
co' li ciampanis a sunin il Mai.

The Day of My Death (first version)

In a city, Trieste or Udine,
        on a street lined with lindens in spring,
colour tingeing the tips of the leaves . . .
        I'll fall dead underneath
        the high, blond, burning sun
                and closing my eyes
I'll leave the sky
to its splendour.

Under a linden turned tepidly green
        I'll fall into the dark of my death
which will scatter the lindens and sun.
        Pretty boys will run out
        through the light
                I've just lost —
They'll be flying out of school
with curls on their brows.

I'll still be young —
        my shirt bright, and my soft hair
like rain showering the sharp dust.
        I'll still be warm —
        and a child bounding by
                on the street's sun-warmed tar
will rest his hand
on my lap of glass.

Il dí da la me muàrt — *La meglio gioventú*
(1941–53)

Ta na sitàt, Trièst o Udin,
   ju par un viàl di tèjs,
di vierta, quan' ch'a múdin
      il colòur li fuèjs,
      i colarài muàrt
sot il soreli ch'al art
            biondu e alt
e i sierarài li sèjs,
lassànlu lusi, il sèil.

Sot di un tèj clípit di vert
      i colarài tal neri
da la me muàrt ch'a dispièrt
      i tèjs e il soreli.
   I bièj zuvinús
a coraràn ta chè lus
            ch'i ài pena pierdút
      svualànt fòur da li scuelis
      cui ris tal sorneli.

Jo i sarài 'ciamò zòvin
      cu na blusa clara
e i dols ciavièj ch'a plòvin
      tal pòlvar amàr.
   Sarài 'ciamò cialt
e un frut curínt pal sfalt
            clípit dal viàl
      mi pojarà na man
      tal grin di cristàl.

Poems by Eaindra and Maung Thein Zaw
Translated from the Burmese by
ko ko thett and James Byrne

Eaindra was born in the Irrawaddy delta in 1973 and is now an 'impermanent resident' in Singapore. Since publishing her first chapbook at twenty Eaindra has become regarded as one of the most outstanding Burmese poets of her generation. She is an active and prolific blogger, contributing to significant Burmese magazines inside and outside Burma. Since 1996, she has published fifty poems and fifteen short stories in print media inside Burma. Her first collected book of poems is imminent and will be published in Rangoon. She is a founding member of the Aesthetic Light Foundation, a charity that aims to promote the wellbeing of Burmese writers inside Burma.

Lily

by Eaindra

Lily flutters her dark wavy eyelashes
From her long ivy hair, from her cheeks, from her neck
A bunch of rainbows bloom in the middle of the night
Her thin top curvy and bent, her minijeans torn and tight
Lily serves beer . . .

Lily cringes more than necessary, Lily comes close more than
    necessary
Lily mixes herself appositely . . . Lily has her own recipe,
    cultures her own yeast
Lily cooks the pose of a shecat in a pencil heel for an
    appetizer . . .
Lily woks the glassbead strings on her pearly breasts into
    munchies . . .
Lily's black irides are like a virgin crow stalking its prey
Lily moves like meatloaf about to be snatched by a hawk
Lily serves beer . . .

Lily promotes beer with her scent
Lily promotes her scent with beer
Lily serves beer . . .

Amid the buzzings of rowdy blowflies
Lusty looks fume as Lily uncorks the syrupy-sweet laughter
    . . . POP! . . .
Lily pours her froth of giggles
To be forked at, gummed and swallowed

With cloudberry lips, Lily serves . . .
Lily's nonchalant smile pierces their stares, Lily serves . . .

Lily knifes words with her gibble-gabble, Lily serves . . .
Lily wants to flow in their arteries, Lily serves . . .

Lily serves like a shaggy she-terrier, cajoling
Lily smashes herself to fit into a bottle for her masters, Lily
    serves

Lily, her face uninterested at the news of homecomings,
Transplants her life branch to branch to serve another
    beer . . .
Lily the bait, Lily the cheery fisherwoman who chaffs . . .
'Life is bitter, life is beer.' Lily serves another beer . . .

'I am God's glitch' she serves . . .
'I am a tiny she-snake from the wickerbasket of the snake
    charmer' she serves

Because it is not bedtime yet...another
Because, on Lily, the nights pour down...another
Dawn unbudded, where the darkness lingers
Where the day is yet to shed new light
Lily serves beer . . .
Lily has just served . . .
Lily is serving . . .

Maung Thein Zaw was born in 1959 to a family of goldsmiths
in Myaing Myo, Pakkokku District, in upper Burma. At fifteen,
he entered the Burmese *zat* performance world as the front man
of a travelling Burmese traditional dance troupe in Mandalay.
His poems have regularly appeared in Burmese magazines since
the 1980s. His poetry, frequently sentimental in its outlook, may
be seen as a reconciliation between the traditional – in terms of
diction, romanticism and philosophy – and the modern, in form.
Two books of his poems, *Dripping Dewdrops* and *Scenery 21*, were
published in one volume in 2008.

the heat bearer

by Maung Thein Zaw

in a not-so-new morning
vivified
in sunshine

i have been infatuated with
that fragrant little ear
of my dream

what a gusty wind

on my heart
a homeless crow is cawing
all my longings are in staccato
i have descended
like a melody who has sobbed herself out of tune
'not really very special' she says

the screechy dry branch
soothes me in magada

having not found a cure under the waterfall
i build a tower the height of my heart
and look out on the genesis of the world

the person who discovered fire happened to be me

magada : the language of nature

Sándor Reményik
'Funeral Oration for the Falling Leaves'
('Halotti beszéd a hulló leveleknek')
Translated from the Hungarian by
Peter V. Czipott and John M. Ridland

A late twelfth-century text known as the 'Funeral Oration' ('Halotti beszéd') is the first surviving complete work in (Old) Hungarian. Its opening is known to every school child in Hungary: 'My brethren, you see with your own eyes what we are: verily, we are dust and ashes.' Several twentieth-century poets used this opening as a point of departure, among them the Transylvanian poet Sándor Reményik (1890-1941). Born in the Hungarian city of Kolozsvár, he wrote most of his works in the Romanian city of Cluj, died in Kolozsvár and lies buried in Cluj-Napoca. He performed this peregrination without ever leaving the city of his birth. With the post-World War I transfer of Transylvania from Hungary to Romania, its ethnic Hungarians went from being a dominant minority to being a subservient one; where the pre-WWI Hungarian policy of Magyarization had suppressed Romanian culture, afterward the roles were reversed. It was in this atmosphere that Reményik became a leading Hungarian poet of Transylvania, concerned with preserving and propagating Hungarian culture. At first glance, his 'Funeral

Oration for the Falling Leaves' would seem to replace the grim
dust and ashes of the original with a more sublime vision of death
as a series of metamorphoses from one form of beauty into the
next. Reményik, however, points to a crucial factor: such sublime
metamorphosis is possible only in one's native environment (he
highlights this with jarringly unrhymed lines that contrast with
the rest of the poem, in which he doesn't shy away even from *rime
riche*). The poem becomes a coded rebuke to those Hungarian
Transylvanians who, seeing no future for themselves in Romanian
society, contemplated or indeed chose emigration.

For a reproduction of the page of the Pray Codex that preserves the
12th-century 'Funeral Oration' and a trilingual (Old Hungarian,
Modern Hungarian, and English) presentation of the complete
text, see http://users.tpg.com.au/etr/oldhu/halotti.html

Funeral Oration for the Falling Leaves

Do you behold, my brethren, what we are?
Verily, scarlet and bronze and golden,
Eternal, holy beauty is what we are.
We cross death's door, fall soundlessly:
Our pomp is greater, verily,
Than this world's senseless pomp can be:
Nothing at all can ever mar
Our true and beautiful selves, our birthright;
Clinging to the tree, we glow in sunlight,
And when we leap to the waiting forest floor,
Brother leaves enclose brother limb, as before.
And there too we are at home, we are at ease.
When we turn brittle, harden, freeze,
Hoar-frost glitters on us, ermine-white.

After the scarlet comes the ermine-white.
Verily, beautiful is what we are.
Do you behold, my brethren, what we are?
When we at last are one with Mother Earth
We also will be as beautiful as the Earth.
We'll also be at home there in the Earth.
My brethren, only one thing orphans us:
To be outside our forest home
Without a homeland, or a home,
Being windswept to and fro
Across the cobblestones of a cold, unfriendly city,
Commingled with all sorts of litter.
My brethren, just that one thing orphans us.
Yet here at home we're what we are:
Verily, scarlet, bronze, and golden,
Eternal, holy beauty is what we are.

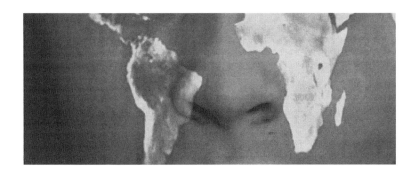

Tomas Venclova
Three poems
Translated from the Lithuanian by Rimas Uzgiris

Tomas Venclova was born in Klaipeda, Lithuania, in 1937, and graduated from Vilnius University. He is a scholar, poet, and translator of literature. Being an outspoken member of the Lithuanian Helsinki Group, which monitored Soviet violations of human rights, Venclova was threatened with a number of sanctions, and was allowed to emigrate in 1977. Since 1980 he has been a member of the department of Slavic Languages and Literatures at Yale University, from which he also received a Ph.D. Collections of his poems have been published in English as *Dialogue in Winter* (1999), and *The Junction: Selected Poems* (2009). He has been the recipient of numerous awards, including the Lithuanian National Prize in 2000 and the 2002 Prize of Two Nations, which he received jointly with Czeslaw Milosz.

Tapestry

Beyond river and stones, the litter of buildings,
There lives a weaving, like slow lightning:

Maiden and beast, lilies and margin,
A mirror's space in the heraldic garden.

It will refresh your mind, drown your pain,
When the pitiless millstones shed their grain,

The parched mouth repeats, 'I can't',
And blood coagulates on the fence's point.

You saw much. Accept the garden, and the sloe.
You will pay up what it is right to bestow:

That day would be justified by the evening to come,
That hardships are hundreds, but music is one.

Slowly opening your eyes . . .

Slowly opening your eyes you see
how staunchly the plaster flatness shines,
and the pillow sags at its frontiers.

You tumble into day. Eyelashes, solidly
pressed cheeks, and clouds, winter, the whine
of a tramway. Again, you begin to see

how time takes apart every stamp and seal,
shores separate from rivers; in your veins
the desert makes a home. Frontiers,

archipelagos, harbours, flatlands – only
sand in an hourglass. A bound and certain
reality. The years left are few. You see

only flashes. Something is born on high,
and touching the pupil like a human alien,
light is stopped at the eyelids' frontiers

still full of the interrupted dream. To testify,
we have the word. With darkness echoing,
something is sketched which we can't see –
the unbeing of, the rhythm of, the sounding of, frontiers.

Commentary

Love language, first of all, even though it's hard to witness
its debasement in newspaper columns, lying obituaries,
    steamy
bedrooms, in complaining typefaces, or the market's clamour,
in trenches, or the reek of wards, in third-rate theatres,

the offices of the interrogator, and on bathroom walls.
Down in the pit of grey buildings, it is guarded
by a staircase's steel net – so that not a person, but an age
should choose when it should be allowed to die –

unravelled here and there, hoarse, littered with ruckus
and rage . . . Still, love language, despite
its exile with us here on earth,
for even in such a state, from out of it shines

the first word, born as in a different universe.
It was given so that we could be distinguished from clay,
from palm and thrush, even perhaps from angels,
so that naming things accurately we could understand them.

Those who try to return to that lost space,
cleaning up language, must understand
that they will, almost certainly, fail. For, as we know,
doors grow more distant faster than we gain.

Its gift is equivalent to losing its power; what is built
will be destroyed without delay. Nor will you walk into
some foreign paradise (there are so many). Having reached it,
you wipe clean your footprints, and lose the key.

Language says, you are only a tool. A power dictates to you,
which, if you look it in the eye, will make you blind.
Or, differently, you will climb Jacob's ladder in a dream,
groping, without a net, straining your powers, lacking
    strength

until someone greets you from above (or not). Pushing you
to the side, at times, he substitutes a few words,
changes the person, improves the syntax, fixes inflection.
This happens quite rarely, but still, it happens,

and then you feel how what you made – is good,
for the letters swim on the page like ice-crystals floating
on a river, and suddenly the bush gets brighter, the shore, the
    city.
Who will read it (if anyone will)? It is not for you to know.

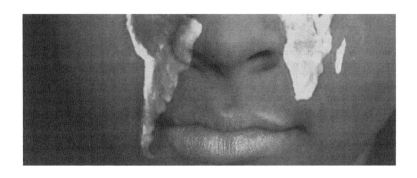

Elżbieta Wójcik-Leese
Three Languages and Three Trees:
Not So False Friends

and if you looked carefully you
saw that there was also
a string from one language to
the other or from the apple tree
to the olive tree

Jean Portante
trans. from the French by Pierre Joris

Trying to discern the string that ties Polish (into which I was born) to Danish (into which I moved two years ago) I search for false friends – words that every translator is supposed to shun. English (my second language) focuses my attention: *more, more,* a Danish child calls comprehensibly. Without fail, sooner than later, the mother – *mor* – replies.

'Polish is *not* a minority language,' says a colleague from the Centre for Internationalisation and Parallel Language Use, questioning my perception of my mother tongue. (The Centre, where I work, was established in 2008 to assist the University of Copenhagen in maintaining the equality of Danish and English – the two languages its academic community lives in, though at times to varying degrees.) 'There are, what, about 36 million Poles?' so argues this representative of a language whose population is six times smaller. I can see his point – against 400 (or so) speakers of Tlingit, the endangered language into which the first ever children's book has just been translated, Polish may seem a global language. Yet, just as Tlingit is now, Polish too was endangered, when Poland was partitioned among Austria, Germany and Russia. I myself had no choice but to learn Russian at school, 60 years after Poland officially regained its independence in 1918.

The realization that Danish enjoyed the same dominance in Scandinavia as Russian in my part of the world, or English elsewhere, came as a surprise during a conversation with the Finnish and Icelandic poets involved in Metropoetica – a poetry-and-translation project (run under the auspices of Literature Across Frontiers) which features five less-widely known languages of Europe, and English as a bridge language.

My surprise well reflected my ignorance about Danish. Before I arrived in Denmark, I had studied Latin, German and French, but it never occurred to me to learn Danish. Yes, I had read Hans Christian Andersen, though in Polish; and Karen Blixen, in English. In English I had also become familiar with the alphabet according to the Dane, Inger Christensen: *apricot trees exist, apricot trees exist*. But I never heard Danish, until two months before my move I switched on the CD player to rehearse the basics, including the Danish alphabet. How strange it sounded – the unfamiliarity intensified by my lack of comprehension: Danish speakers swallow a half of every word, whereas Poles pronounce every single letter.

After one month in Danish, I flew to Riga for a week of Metropoetica workshops. Latvian seemed closer than Danish, also because of the recognizable ambivalence of Russian's imposed vicinity. When I boarded the plane to return to my new home, however, I was astonished how Danish insisted aurally on its familiarity.

Riga – Copenhagen

boarding the plane jeg forstår
the hub bub of the language
not yet quite familiar

the Latvian quickly recedes behind
hvad hedder det? what's that?

the glottal stop, the in-drawn ja
and the mental nod
of partial recognition

shift an accent by one notch
and another
language nudges itself into
the intonation
of this flight

In a Danish course I soon practised the glottal stop, imitated by
the split /hub bub/, and the soft /d/, which renders the typically
doubled expression of happiness, *meget meget glad*, into a phrase
of 'glad *mal*functioning'. Unfortunately, the teacher favoured
grammar translation; the endless repetition of 'I have lost my
jacket' made me search for my own passages into Danish. I
bought Inger Christensen's *Samlede Digte* and every existing
English translation of the individual collections that compose
this volume.

Sure enough, on page 393 *abrikostræerne findes, abrikostræerne
findes*. On page 49 I found the poem 'Gry,' whose title I could
readily understand – the Polish *gry* means *games* in English.
What does it mean in Danish?

Dusk. The games of dusk then. *Gry i zabawy zmroku*, I jotted
down in Polish. And I was hooked: if I could find, if there could
be found, *findes*, more words to string together in order to join

one tree to another tree, one language to the other. I started
looking for more such not-so-false friends.

Dusk and shade. In my new northern motherland these two are
not particularly welcome. Danes relish light and sun – naturally,
as both are scarce here. Danes seem (to me) to mercilessly trim
their trees or, even worse, to fell them in order to invite more
light. In Kraków, in front of my window, grew an oak tree:
my nation, as daring as an oak, a Polish poet concluded once. In
København, in front of my window, grew an acacia tree. But it
was felled. I chose to celebrate its presence in all my languages
simultaneously. Single words – triple false friends – helped to tie
the string. The Danish for *leaves* is *blade*, which means *blade* in
Polish (that is, *pale* in English) and the *blade* is English as well.

In-sights

and if I lean close enough
I can see the finest of cuts
the acacia tree left here

now eight months absent
fældes from the fælles have
where it leaned against our window

the slanting trunk found our glass
to steady its precarious weight
of flint blades, leaves
sharpened by northern sun
to their incisive paleness

True friends exist. False friends may become true.

Launch of 'Polyphony', *MPT* 3/14 at St. Martin-in-the-Fields

On Thursday 24th March 2011 *MPT* held a celebration of our Autumn 2010 issue, 'Polyphony', at St. Martin-in-the-Fields, Trafalgar Square, London.

Reading from 'Polyphony' were Steve Komarnyckyj, Emily Jeremiah, Tim Allen, and *MPT*'s editors David and Helen Constantine. There was also jazz from Tony Baker and Liz Hanaway, who interpreted a number of poems featured in the issue.

Tim Allen

Steve Komarnyckyj

Tony Baker and
Liz Hanaway

Emily Jeremiah

Photos: Deborah de Kock

Reading at Free the Word Festival

On April 6th 2011 an evening of readings from *MPT*, was the opening event of the *Free the Word! Festival.*

Stephen Watts, Sasha Dugdale, Martina Thomson, Chris Beckett and Michael Foley, together with David and Helen Constantine, explored the theme of *MPT*'s Spring 2011 issue *Poetry and the State*, through a diverse selection of readings. Together they examined poetry's ability to defend and celebrate a common humanity world-wide. This event was organised in partnership with English PEN, and held at the Free the Word Centre in Farringdon.

David Constantine

Martina Thomson

Chris Beckett

Photos: Sakia Schmidt / English PEN

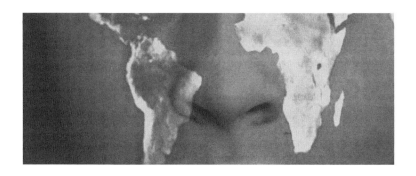

Baudelaire
(from) 'The Poor Child's Toy',
Le Spleen de Paris IX
Translated from the French by Michael Rosen

On a road and behind the railings of a vast garden – at the end of which there appeared a handsome chateau, white in the sun – stood a beautiful, fresh-looking child in his charming country clothes.

The luxury, the carefree style and the usual display of wealth makes one think that pretty children like this are made of a material different from ordinary or poor children.

Next to him on the grass lay a splendid toy, as fresh-looking as its master, varnished and golden, wearing a purple dress and covered in feathers and glass beads. But the child wasn't interested in his favourite toy – this was what he was looking at:

> on the other side of the railings, on the road, amongst the thistles and nettles, there was another child who was filthy, sickly and covered in soot. He was one of those despised brats in whom an unprejudiced eye could find beauty – just as the expert's eye can find a perfect painting beneath a coach-maker's varnish – so long as he cleaned off the awful patina of poverty.

Through these symbolic bars, dividing the two worlds of the main road and the chateau, the poor child was showing his toy to the rich one, who was studying it as avidly as if it were a rare, unknown object. Yet this toy, which the little ragamuffin was annoying and bothering and shaking in its cage, was a live rat! The child's parents, no doubt for reasons of economy, had taken the toy from the living world.

And the two children were laughing together, one to the other, in a brotherly sort of a way, revealing teeth which were *equally* white.

Thomas Rosenlöcher, Heiner Müller, Thomas Brasch
Poems translated from the German by Ken Cockburn

Born in Dresden in 1947, Thomas Rosenlöcher lived in the GDR until reunification in 1990. He first completed a commercial training before studying at the Johannes R. Becher Literature Institute in Leipzig. He has worked as a freelance author since 1983, and is a member of the Saxon Academy of Arts. Based in Dresden, he is currently writer-in-residence for Bergen-Enkheim, a district of Frankfurt-am-Main. 'Die Distel' is from his first book, published in the GDR in 1982, and is included in *Das Flockenkarussell* (Suhrkamp 2007), a collection of new and selected poems.

The Thistle

Far off I saw the zigzag chimney-smoke
drift down. But warbling overhead and somer-
saulting soared a lark. Oh just be quiet.
Power strides towards power. And those
who lack power hobble on as best they can.

That's how I thought. A thistle though stood tall,
made graceful by its spiky filigree,
and thoroughly ennobled by its purple,
breaking the stone. Around it were arranged
such landscape, field and hill the place contained,
and wherever I made for, there it stood again.
I knew then, even if the powers-that-be
used dynamite to fence off the horizon,
it moves beneath, the lion's silent sister,
beneath the concrete, occupying the field.
The time will come. The storeys of the dark
must give their feathered herbage teeth
and, burdock bristling everywhere about,
rise up into their miracle of flower,
so glimmers carry even to the depths.

Heiner Müller (1929–1995) lived in the GDR through its forty-
year history, moving in and out of favour with the authorities,
though by the 1980s his international standing had secured
him a measure of independence in his homeland. He was, like
Brecht, best known in his lifetime as a playwright who paralleled
this public activity with the writing of poems. These were first
collected in 1992 as *Gedichte 1949-1989* (Alexander Verlag 1992),
and arranged by decade ('1949 . . .', '1959 . . .', etc). 'NAPOLEON
ZUM BEISPIEL' comes towards the end of the opening section,
'1949 . . .', and was first published in 1975.

NAPOLEON FOR INSTANCE wept at Wagram
As his Imperial Guard made their escape
Over their own who lay there wounded and
the wounded cried out VIVE L'EMPEREUR.
The monument was touched: his mortar cried.
One Sunday, work completed, he, LENIN,
set out to hunt for hares, with, as a guide
his driver, otherwise without companions.

This his leisure. Into the woods he walked
alone. The driver namely had to stay
beside the car, that was indispensable.
Lenin met a peasant in the woods
out gathering mushrooms. Hunting, put aside.
The old man cursed the Soviet powers-that-be
Within his village, Haves and Have-nots still.
All talk, little bread. The mushrooms scarce as well.
Laughed, when Lenin wrote down his complaints
The village, the comrades' names and their mistakes.
He had already complained. And more than once.
Who are we. Say for instance you were Lenin
And Lenin were a man like you who listens
Belief would still be possible in change
But you're not Lenin so things stay as they are.

Thomas Brasch (1945–2001) grew up in the German Democratic
Republic. A protest over the 1968 Soviet invasion of Czechoslovakia
led to a brief prison term, and in 1976, when it became clear he
could not publish in the GDR, he moved to West Berlin, finding
immediate success with his short stories, plays, poems and films.
The poem is from his 1980 collection *Der schöne 27. September*
(The Glorious 27th September, Suhrkamp 1980); Droyenstrasse
is a street in the upmarket Charlottenburg district of what was
West Berlin.

A Nazi Wipes the Hallway

clean: Droyenstrasse 1. He creeps upstairs over
the linoleum with his bucket: Two years
SS-Standard Adolf Hitler, six years iron ore
in Workuta. Each step individually and every wrinkle. So
who is it makes history. I am responsible,

oh yes, appointed by the owner of the house. Who gets
a key for the lift, I decide. For
a minimum pension and rent-free accommodation. Because
I too was guilty, but not in the pay of the state. Just ask
my wife. She hanged herself thirty years ago
with good reason. Now she sits downstairs on the couch
drinking, her own husband a janitor. Don't
you understand: shoes off. Or
should I start again from the beginning.

(For more translations by Ken Cockburn of Brasch and
Rosenlöcher see *MPT* 3/6 and 3/11.)

Stuart Henson
Pushkin Variations

One of the joys of the second-hand bookshop is the anticipation of finding some little out-of-print treasure that will lead you down a new pathway or back to an old one with renewed enthusiasm. Last summer I was delighted to come across an attractive Penguin Poets selection of Pushkin from the 1960s with prose translations and introduction by John Fennell, which was the immediate inspiration for these Variations. For someone who can neither speak nor read Russian, the combination of the mysterious Cyrillic text and the discreet prose translations at the foot of the page is an ideal starting-point. Then it was really a case of just having a go – trying to make a new, living poem with an honest relation to Pushkin's original.

In the appendix to his *Orpheus* Don Paterson makes a very useful distinction between translations and versions, which, while they have the original to serve as a detailed ground-plan and elevation, are 'trying to build a robust home in a new country'. Following his principles in these versions, I have tried to be faithful to the basic structure of each poem whilst allowing myself a certain latitude with contemporary diction. So there are some images that Pushkin might not have recognised, but no ideas, I hope, that he would feel were out of place.

The water nymph

Alone, where the lake laps at the root
of ancient alders, peat-steeped oaks,
the anchorite, praying, starving, praising,
scoops out his own grave, pausing
at last to look right through the sunset
to the throne of God, his heart molten,
his soul infatuated now with holy fear.

Meanwhile the black horizon seems
to suck all daylight from the cloud,
the wood silts up and the moon
draped only in her bloodied rags
draws vapours from the lake-top
like a mist of mayflies rising
and boiling on the brooding air.

Then, as he gazes on the mirror-face,
the drowned sky shudders and his sweat
dries cold. Out of the hidden moil
a girl shines upward from the depth, slipping
weed silks from shoulder, breast, hip . . .
turning to lie, hair spread and legs astride
the rock that outcrops on the farther shore.

Her stare is deeper than desire: it says
swim to me if you dare; I am the pool,
the spawning-place. Give up. Confess
and I'll absolve your body's torture.
And when he groans she knows and smiles
and plunges back into the water,
silver and instant as a shooting-star.

Prayer is a lost cause. All the next day
his spirit whores among a hundred
shifting images of her. Will she be there
when the moon crawls slowly
from the sagging shades and shapes
that congregate at dusk beyond the lake
to watch him watching from his door?

And yes, she comes and mocks him
once and one night more, flaunting
her ferny loins and splashing, calling
the monk with pouts and tearful eyes
and little chastely breathless sighs,
only to dive and leave him sunk and shaken,
haunted by the pretty trickle of her laughter.

Three nights; two lead-weight dawns.
The fourth morning ash-wraiths
skitter from his fire and the monk's door keens
on its hinge. Nikolai and Dimitri, fishing,
hook in the mealed corpse, the tangled beard,
the sackcloth rolling where the currents
swell across the lake's uneven floor.

Arion

The decks were swarmed with mariners:
slaves hauling the sheets in,
boys crawling like spiders in the rigging,
the power-house plunging the great oars
in the foam, and calm in that storm
of action our silent helmsman, setting course

for home on a dead-reckoning.
And me, naturally, with my art, my poetry,
my happy heart, my off-key singing . . .
Before the tornado tore us apart.
Survivors? You must be joking!
Oarsman, hands, helmsman, lost to a man.
No one but me, ringing out my soaking shirt,
humming a line from a new verse,
unhurt, with my bum in the sun-dried sand.

After Pushkin

Caught in the clatter of a city street,
or stepping through the still hush of a church,
or at a gig, maybe, crushed in the mosh-pit,
my mind plays God, reminding me that each

of us must pass into the world of darkness
when the years run down his little store of light.
Among the hundreds there who push and press
one may be due to stage-dive out tonight.

Look at that oak. My father climbed that tree's
green limbs, and so did I; yet every spring
when I'm gone it will delete those memories
and burn a brand new summer in its rings.

Even to hold a baby is to take
the time-bomb of the future in your hands.
He sleeps now, all potential. When he wakes
his expectations detonate my end.

Each day I turn the diary's page – another
week, another month, a year – I try to guess
which is my last; when will the calendar
mark nothing but the blank space of my death.

And sometimes, too, I stop and wonder *where?*
Out on a lake, caught by a freakish wave?
Maybe the innocent victim of a war
I didn't make, flung in a hasty grave?

My corpse won't care. But still, let it be near
the places that I learned to love – one
corner of some local field; a space where kids
make-out, and new shoots break, warmed by the sun.

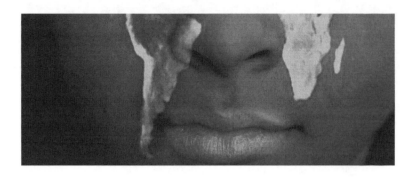

Yang Jian
Three poems
Translated from the Chinese by
Fiona Sze-Lorrain

Born in Anhui Province in 1967, **Yang Jian** (杨键) worked as a factory labourer for thirteen years and began writing poetry during the mid-80s. Laureate of the 1st Liu Li'an Poetry Award (1995), the 9th Rougang Poetry Award (2000), the 1st Yulong Poetry Award (2006), as well as the prestigious Chinese Media Literature Award (2008), his books of poetry include *Dusk* (2003), rated as one of the top ten national poetry titles of the year; *Ancient Bridge* (2007) and *Remorse* (2009). Considered today as one of the greatest Chinese living poets, Yang Jian also paints with ink and brush. He leads a Buddhist life in Ma'anshan, Anhui.

Mount Zhen Monastery

How relaxed the banana tree looks
A dog leaps, biting at its fleas
Tired of barking, it'll sleep

A little girl flips over lotus leaves
Her brother carries a bucket of water to the vegetables
Mountains stretch like an open *kasaya*

Peasants dig in a garlic field
Light pours in
This is how the dead are blessed

Mud from the bottom of the pond
lies by the road
We live in a great age of exposure

Ancient Departure

They come, they go
A century where man lives in shame of his kindness
I step upon dust, this old wife
still guards her pagoda, a healthy voice

They come, they go
Our eyes grow sore from yearnings
Embrace disappearance, learn to see how the moon glows
Wind of the heart shifts rivers and mountains

They come, they go
When passions die
how blue the sky will be
We rise and fall in transparency, understand strength in
    stillness

They come, they go
I watch you in light wind
I'm tired, even mountains can't inspire me
Speaker of the sunset, is he the sunset?

Romance in Life and Death

A man's life after death
is the memory of him by the living –
Long after his death
the mirror he used opens its mouth and speaks
the chair he sat on starts to mumble
even the path misses his footsteps

Outside the window
the slow flute notes and the slow setting sun
are the familiar tone he used
A living man's life
is the memory of a dead man –

After a long time
a living man will speak and act
just like the dead

Tristan Corbière
'Dead Men's Casino'
Translated from the French by
Christopher Pilling

With the appearance of his image on the new €0.75 postage stamp, Tristan Corbière (1845–75) has been recognised at last as a major French poet. He saw himself as a sailor manqué, 'furiously in love with the sea, on which he only sailed in stormy weather', as Verlaine put it in *Les poètes maudits*. A considerable section of poems in his only collection, *Les Amours jaunes*, lauded sailors ('this gruff and sinewy tribe . . . who die with their boots on') so his imaginary Casino is situated by the actual Dead Men's Bay (Baie des Trépassés, in Brittany near La Pointe du Raz). He went to live in Roscoff where he wrote most of his poems, and had a boat to sleep in beside his dog, as well as one to risk life and limb in at sea. This Casino was published in *La Vie parisienne* in 1875, and not again until 1941 in Algiers. Parts bear a strong resemblance to the 'old nunnery' in 'Poet by default' ('Le poète contumace') – one of his finest poems, which he would also have you believe he wrote in Penmarc'h, where the Tristan of legend waited in vain for Yseut. This suited him as he could be on his own, the lover manqué.

DEAD MEN'S CASINO

A country, – no, it's the harsh broken coastline and rock-strewn
slopes of Brittany: *Penmarc'h, Toul-Infern, Poul-Dahut, Stang-
an-Ankou*... Barbarous names blared by squalls and flurries
of wind, rolled under the muffled swell of the waves, broken
in the breakers and lost in goosepimples on the marshes . . .
Names that have voices.

There, beneath a neutral sky, the tempest is in her element: the
lull is a time to mourn.

There, under a leaden expanse of water, lies the town of Ys, the
drowned Sodom.

There lies *Dead Men's Bay* from whose depths the bones of ship-
wrecked sailors return to rap on the doors of every shack to beg a
winding-sheet; and the *Raz-de-Sein,* criss-crossed by currents no
man has ever sailed through without fear or misfortune.

There, creatures the colour of the rockface are born and
die, patient as eternal beings, hiccupping a poor, almost dead
language, unfitted for laughter or weeping . . .

That's where I invent a casino.

DEAD MEN'S CASINO

(WINTER STOPOVER)
THE OPEN ARMS FOR THE OUT OF PLUCK
FOR HORSE-RIDERS & FOOT-SLOGGERS

It's an old belfry, still upright but with its horns trimmed. Its
spire is at its feet – where it fell. Tumbledown cottages flung
drunkenly against it in heaps are sheltered from the incoming
tides and the close-shaving gusts of wind.

The thing is, it's a good tower, solid enough for bells and
culverins, those five hundredweight cannons, and strong enough
to withstand time and weather; a former hidey-hole for Knights
Templar, and what good workers in the service of God they were!
Hallowed pillars of the temple and the guardroom. On entering

you can still breathe that indefinable smell of consecrated stone that never goes away.

The interior consists of a square well with four bare walls. Half-way up, a long deep-set ogive-slit lets in a ray of light. The breeze buzzes up there like a caged bluebottle. Every so often little black openings climb these interior walls: they go with the steps winding up within their thickness; at every landing alcoves have been built, each with a bull's eye looking out to the horizon. This is where our guests will lodge.

Cellular lay-out: twelve foot square, whitewashed walls, fine chestnut window ledges, Christ's Passion nails as coat-hooks; a nun's palliasse, a stone trough for ablutions, a telescope, a blunderbuss primed with buckshot for ducks or *Philistines*. And that's it.

At ground level, in the nave paved with tombstones, the kitchen – an all-purpose kitchen. – You can enter on horseback. – There's an alchemist's oven, a fireplace as large as a small cottage, big enough to accommodate a ship's masts (for – God willing – a stretch of sand is as good as a forest that's regularly felled); and firedogs from hell for burning bladder-wrack.

Ensconced under the chimney-breast: wooden stools for good old Homer, Doctor Faust, Parson Rabelais, Jean Bart who put the fear of God into Dutch and English alike, Saint Anthony, Job the Leper and other ancients who live on, and a hole for the crickets, should they want one. A night-torch rammed near the trammel; everywhere clamps – for hanging the clog that holds matches, the box for salt, the sausages made of chitterlings, the palm-branches, the waxed boots, and a horseshoe for good luck.

Against the smoke-stained wall, weapons and harness for the chase, fishing and hunting with hounds: duck-guns, harpoons, nets, pewter dishes, copper pans, lanterns. At the door, the execution block; in the centre, a real *dolmen* for revelries, surrounded by stiff armchairs shaped like guillotines. Hoisted on the ceiling beams are battens for outsize still lifes. In the corner, in *chiaroscuro*, a free-standing cuckoo-clock in a good oak coffin, tolling the knell of the hours. Quite filling the huge font, a family of electric cats; below, a plump pug on a turnspit growls, and hobbling about, hither and thither, waddle odd-looking ducks.

At the top, on a simple cathedral-like elevation, level with the giant window, we will have the sole storey, a wooden platform erected to form a sort of *bell-loft*. Access will be by a narrow spiral staircase or by a ship's guy-ropes rigged with ratlines to a maintop platform that serves as landing. That's the workshop – *Studio di far-niente*.

Daylight is adjusted at will by the curtains from a theatre that hasn't made ends meet. In the middle, a monumental table strewn with papers; under it, sealskins. All around, Persian divans. On the walls, harlequin wall-hangings, tapestries, hand-coloured calfskin, battered sails, flags, splendidly sordid tatters. Scraps of stock Épinal prints still stuck to the door. Facing you, a Russian cooking range and the kettle for making tea. At the rear, a chapel organ for barrel-organists, and recesses for superannuated saints. A large canvas on a stretcher for painters to dump their rubbish. A stove-in rowing-boat full of fresh hay for dogs and poets. A camp bed: philosophers above it and two little black pigs below. Nearby a tobacconist's kiosk. In the space remaining, hammocks slung like spiders' webs in the midst of gymnastic apparatus. Attached to a well-chain, hooked up so high it's out of sight, sways the chandelier, a real grappling-iron forged by a fuzzled farrier, who's a virgin still.

Higher up, as high as can be climbed, is the outside gallery and, overlooking the whole region, an open platform washed by rainstorms, swept by whirlwinds, pockmarked by moonlight. A rusty weathercock pecks away at itself, impaled on the lightning conductor.

Little gardens clog the gargoyle gutter-spouts. At the quoins two machicolated gateways gape over the abyss and two pinnacles point a finger at the sky.

One will be rigged as a lookout post: a telegraph mast with

fantastic big arms and a demented belfry that sudden upsurges of wind will set ringing, on gala nights, when there's a wreck to plunder.

The other, also waiting for a chance wind . . . will wait.

There, I want small dark leaded windows with grills, impenetrable in the tall barbican, bristling with clusters of iron spikes; a secret iron gate studded with nails, reinforced with bolts . . . and wide open.

I want the oubliette to be aerial, lined with pompadour pattern flowerets, chock-a-block with flowers in bloom; a stuffed canary in a gilded cage, a larger than life Murano mirror, a Crébillon sofa and a domed ceiling painted by Mahomet (7th manner) . . .

All this is for the poor wreck up in the air, the strolling woman of dreams, the grey shadow who gallops away like the dead in ballads . . . going but never coming. The Duchess of Marlborough, perhaps:

'Anne, sister Anne, do you see nothing coming? — Nothing! Nothing but the hurricane skirling, the weathervane whirling, the dense mist swirling . . .'

DEAD MEN'S CASINO

Oh! the wild high life that will be lived there, my lords, guests of this establishment!

A1 HOSTELRY FOR THE OUT OF PLUCK

To hell with everything!

Oh! a hearty tatie-pot to buck us up! Oh! we're great if we fill our lungs and speak out! what elegant cynicism! forgetting is healing, and forty winks spell release! . . .

Give us the freedom to be alone together in groups, each of us inspired, each kept apart by the strong breeze that blows dry seaweed and empty seashells away.

Here, our means allow us to be poor.

No run-of-the-mill fellow to spoil our countryside, our sea and our desert. Brothers, here's your uniform, soft felt hat, brown shirt in Capuchin cloth, sailcloth breeches, fawn leather sea-boots. We can strut, can't we?

Huntsmen, you can keep your great stretches of sand and marshland; sailors, keep the pretty pretty sea and its fish given to dining on fishermen; here come your whaling boats in white cedar wood, gallant vessels hoisted onto their iron brackets under the porch.

Here are our crews for the occasion: shipmates o' the coast, old rough-necks, porpoise-like pilots, whole-hog cooks and chambermaids . . .

Landlubbers, bury yourselves in your cottages. And the rest of you, stay put in prison cells, nest in eyries, perch in the shrouds!

And no witticisms, please: we're sober of speech once we've understood one another.

You, lazybones, write a book – everyone has a book in him – and ennui will bend over and soothe you. Got up as a painter, slough off the old style. O harpist! stop harping on and listen! Rhymester, emptied of rhymes, here come the haunted hours . . .

Let's breathe the air that inebriates . . . ! And you who are heartsick of living, come and hide your head here, and lie back on the salty turf, having cancelled your subscription to life.

Tristan.

Penmarc'h. – September.

Reviews

Ikinci Yeni : The Turkish Avant-Garde
Edited and Translated by George Messo
Shearsman Books
168 pp, ISBN 101-8-4861-066-1

Poetry has always been the dominant art form in Turkish culture but in the 20th century both Turkish politics and poetry were to be transformed in the crucible of a modernist revolution that strove to erase the past and rewrite the future. The Kemalist Turkish Republic in 1923 introduced a language revolution, which sought to streamline, simplify and 'purify' Turkish, to rid it of its Farsi and Arabic Ottoman court finery. A new phonetic Latin alphabet brought mass literacy, and instantly made the past unreadable. As in the Soviet Union, poets in the new Turkish Republic had a symbiotic and problematic relationship with the State. Nazim Hikmet, Turkey's foremost modernist poet, was to die in exile in Moscow. The first wave of Turkish avant-garde poetics, the *Garip* poets, produced limpid and often magical work, Orhan Veli's 'Rag and Bone Man' for instance, which sought to strip poetry of its artifice, literary techniques and conventions, to write transparent direct language that spoke to the people. Unfortunately the exuberant surrealist and politically engaged verse the *Garip* movement produced was as short-lived as Veli himself, who died prematurely at the age of thirty-six. Critics soon detected a darker, more introspective, abstract and individualistic turn in modern Turkish poetry, which they labelled the *Ikinci Yeni*, the Second New.

Messo chooses to open his spirited and idiosyncratic introduction to the movement theatrically with 'Phaeton', Ece Ayhan's seductively decadent death-wish of a poem, which embodies many of the formal and thematic concerns thought to distinguish the *Ikinci Yeni* literary movement: allusive and elusive verse which plays fugitive games with the unconscious, evades clarity, refuses the definitive, defers meaning and accedes to dream-logic. Brittle melancholy loneliness plays on an old gramophone as a suicidal black phaeton rides through Pera's 'streets of deathly love', past shop window displays of montenegro pistols wrapped in tulle, oleander photographs and Algerian violets in a showcase. Ayhan concludes that the presence of the horse-drawn phaeton, its rise to the heavens, 'could be down to my sister choosing to buy the Algerian violets'. The tropes of the city, of loneliness, of dream-like encounter and surreal juxtaposition in Ayhan's poem ripple throughout the collection.

Unlike the Garip poets of the first wave of modernist Turkish poetry, the Second New poets all rejected the idea of being part of a movement and had no sense of collective identity, no manifesto and refused the literary characterisations ascribed to them. The Second New poets' linguistic experimentalism reflected a search for a new epistemology. Messo characterises this experimentalism as 'hermetic, ruminative, subversive – an implosive resistance to the naïve, delusional "open" language of a closed state.' Whilst his story is, as he asserts, canonical in Turkish literary circles, this collection provides us with an intoxicating introduction to the ghosts that haunted the five most renowned Second New poets, and continue to haunt the Turkish literary imagination today.

Istanbul is a recurrent presence in the collection. The city had been a traditional locus for the Divan poetry of the previous century but the poetry of the Ottoman court had been written in a different alphabet, a different language, and its poets had celebrated the glories of a city of rose gardens, mosques and minarets. In contrast this first generation of poets born after the birth of the Republic, frequented the seamier, shabbier corners of a city shrouded in melancholy. Here in Uyar's 'One Day, Early in the Morning':

And yet, fog still lingers on the Golden Horn,
There's the echo of ferry horns.
Twilight everywhere,
The bridge is still up.

There is a constant contrast between the shadowy chiaroscuro of
ferries, railway stations, tram stops, dilapidated ghetto bars and
lokantas in the labyrinthine backstreets of Galata and Pera, the grimy
glamour and decaying grandeur of Istanbul's European quarter and
the protean brilliance of the sea, roiling with wriggling squid and
octopus, smelling of fish and tar. The city, so often characterised as
a bridge between the East and West, dissolves, becomes cloud, rain,
fog, a stream of consciousness. Deterritorialised memories and echoes
drift across continents and time zones , as in Berk's London poem 'The
Thames':

> At night I'm out to Piccadilly sitting on a stone
>   flushing a pigeon into flight
> I break a glass with a black man in a bar and stare
>   long and hard at a woman, at a twisting road and
> I take up the Thames and go, then perhaps it's another river, the
>   Bosphorous
> (so it's the Bosphorus and Asafpasha mansion, its divans and delicate
>   curtains
> a canary – from the Philippines, yellow, it never sings or else the
> canary I'm looking at
>   is a window – the interiors of dark rooms, lanterns,
>   kitchen hands (mostly Armenian), the men's room, frying
>   pans, plates, knives and forks and lamps, fuses, maces,
>   brazier coals, administrators, the little woman, a key, robes
>   and
>   jackets.

Rimbaud, Baudelaire, Nerval, Breton, Eliot and Éluard's visions
of the city haunt these poems, and the sense of being in the wake
of European modernisms is strong. It would be easy to dismiss the
Turkish avant-garde as parochial; after all it's 1958 when Ayhan's
ghostly hearse glides through Galata. However the reader familiar
with Turkish history will be aware there are other ghosts at play. The
sadness that pervades these poems owes as much to the centuries-old
Islamic tradition of *huzun* and to the contemporary political traumas
of the Menderes era, as to European Romantic poetic melancholy or
Surrealist nostalgia. This is an Istanbul haunted by the ghosts of its
Greek inhabitants, expelled from Istanbul in 1955; of a people haunted
by the ghosts of a centuries-old multicultural, multilingual Empire

now rendered foreign and incomprehensible. At its best the poetry of
the Second New provides us with glimpses of a subtle epistemology
which evokes this haunting and evades crass political certainties. As
Cansever puts it in 'It was the Jazz Season':

> And it was strange, even remembering
> Was remembering
> Borrowing from the future
> And that was a cause of happiness
> A reason for unhappiness
> As if a perfectly unique garden
> From the peak of non-existence
> Had come down piece by piece.

Alev Adil

Indian Poetry in Translation

K. Sachidanandan
While I Write: New and Selected Poems, translated from
Malayalam by the poet
Harper Collins, India; 2011
ISBN: 978-93-5029-038-5; Price: Rs299

The Rapids of a Great River: The Penguin Book of Tamil Poetry,
Edited by Lakshmi Holmström, Subashree Krishnaswamy and
K. Srilata
Penguin, India; 2009
ISBN: 978-0-67-008281-0; Price: Rs499

Interior Decoration:
Poems by 54 women from 10 languages,
Edited by Ammu Joseph, Vasanth Kannabiran, Ritu Menon,
Volga
Women Unlimited, India; 2010
ISBN: 81-88965-62-6; Price: Rs395

Since Vedavyasa (author of *Mahabharata*) and Valmiki (author of *Ramayana*), poetry has formed an integral part of India's cultural life. Even the popular Hindi film songs are written by some of India's finest lyricists. The numbers of poets writing in the various Indian languages bear testimony to poetry's appeal, though publication outlets remain limited. Sales are confined to readers in the respective languages as translations are hard to come by. The publishing industry in English is growing by leaps and bounds in India. But translations of the vast treasury of Indian poetry have yet to benefit from this trend.

Indian novelists writing in English have clearly made their mark. The fact, however, remains that no Indian writer, apart from Rabindranath Tagore, has been awarded the Nobel Prize. The book that won Tagore the prize, *Gitanjali* (1912), contained his own re-creations in poetic prose in English of verses from the original Bengali *Gitanjali* (1910). Tagore was not awarded the prize for his considerable achievements as a poet in Bengali. Poets writing in Indian languages often translate their work into English. K. Sachidanandan (1946-), who writes in Malayalam, is one such example. The translation scene in India today looks promising. The three books reviewed here reflect the sheer diversity, excellence and vibrancy of the writings/translations on offer.

Sachidanandan's poetry is an irresistible mix of the real, surreal, intellectual, sensual, spiritual. By way of introduction (p. ix), he writes: 'My mother taught me to talk to cats and crows and trees; from my pious father I learnt to communicate with gods and spirits. My insane grandmother taught me to create a parallel world in order to escape the vile ordinariness of the tiringly humdrum everyday world; the dead taught me to be one with the soil; the wind taught me to move and shake without ever being seen and the rain trained my voice in a thousand modulations. With such teachers, perhaps it was impossible for me not to be a poet, of sorts.' Sachidanandan read the great Malayalam fiction writers and poets, as well as translations of Tagore, Bankim, Saratchandra and Tarasankar along with Tolstoy, Dostoevsky, Hugo, Zola, Maupassant, Flaubert and Mann among others. He also read the Bible, the *Mahabharata*, Buddha's *Dhammapada* and *The Communist Manifesto*. This 'internationalism' and awareness of world literatures and philosophy is as evident in Tagore (1861-1941) as among contemporary poets.

Sachidanandan does not shy away from asking the deeper existential questions – of being, freedom, love, compassion, nature, language, death. In 'Nero's Soliloquy' (based on his visit to the Forum in Rome), he pleads: 'I can't stand cruelty except my own./ I am the lyric poet,/ my lyre my only refuge./ Please don't wrest this from me./ This city is burning like any other,/ in the fire of its own sins./ Let it burn and let me play.' Poetry may make nothing happen; for Sachidanandan, poetry 'is a shared mother tongue of human beings that survived the Babel. No wonder it has survived Plato's Republic, Hitler's Auschwitz and Stalin's Gulag, and still whispers its uneasy truths into the human ear . . . It rises up from the ocean of the unsayable to name the nameless and to give a voice to the voiceless . . . The truths it discovers may not often be of immediate use, but it will gradually become part of social consciousness' (p. xvii).

In 'Mon Amour', a poem dedicated to Alan Resnais' film, *Hiroshima Mon Amour*, the impossibility of speaking about the horrors of Hiroshima is captured in the sexual metaphor set against the background of the holocaust: 'I hug you with my eyes/ you caress me with your wounds/ I peel off your garments/ you wipe off your bloodstains/ I suck your lips/ your acid burns mine/ I taste your tongue/ your untold tales sour my mouth/ I rouse your nipples/ you mourn your estranged son/ I run my fingers across your belly/ you start as if recalling a rape/ I play on your behind/ it grows heavy with distances/ I press my lips on your petals/ you remind me of your orphaned kids/ I enter you/ you scream like an embattled city/ I raise you to the rainbows/ you climax in a rain of bombs/ I break and scatter in you/ my shrapnels pierce you// Love bleeds in prisons.' One forgets this poem is a translation; it has all the power of an original. The language is pared down to essentials; the poem's message is universal.

The Rapids of a Great River is an anthology of Tamil poems in translation, selected from a rich history of nearly two thousand years of poetry, beginning with the Sangam poets of the 2nd century C.E. The first poem, 'To Tirumal', reads like a hymn: 'In words, you are the truth./ Among virtues, you are love.' Language, thought and emotion come together with striking effect. In *Tirukkural*, the down-to-earth, pithy aphorisms remind us of Proverbs: 'Good friends are like good books –/ A perpetual delight.' They delight us with their elegance and wit, graphic metaphors and wordplay.

Between the sixth and ninth centuries, 'Bhakti' poetry or songs of love addressed to God, transformed Tamil literature and society. But the directness of their poetry can be traced to Sangam times with its 'akam' (inner world/ love poetry), and 'puram' (outside/ public poetry). 'I knew nothing about love, / but you came seeking after me/ in my innocent days/ and aroused my longing for you. // I lost myself in desire/ and hankered after your grace' (Tayumanavar). This 'drama in miniature' is in the 'akam' mode, while a brilliant descriptive passage – 'There waves roar from waterfalls, scattering their pearls, / spreading along the courtyards, washing away toy-houses. / There we collect wild honey and dig for tubers, / . . . / there we pound our gathered grain with rogue elephants' tusks. / There monkeys throw and catch sweet mangoes as if they were playthings/ and the honeyed scent of shenbagam flowers explodes in the skies' (from Kuttrala Kuravanci) – with its sharpness of imagery reminds us of 'puram' poems.

It is not till the late 1980s and 1990s that we encounter new voices in Tamil poetry – Sri Lankan, women and Dalit (the former untouchables), among others. These poets are not afraid of writing with brutal honesty about their concerns – be it marriage, motherhood, sex, caste, war, power, literary canons and aesthetics. A new Sri Lankan Tamil identity is affirmed in poets like R. Cheran (1960-). In 'I could forget everything', he captures the nightmarish quality of the civil war in Sri Lanka, the deep sense of loss and violation by stacking up memories, each detail a poignant re-enactment of the horrors of war: 'I could forget all this,/ . . . // But you, my girl,/ snatched away and burnt/ . . . / as you waited in secret/ while the handful of rice/ – found after so many days – / cooked in its pot/ your children hidden beneath the tea bushes/ . . . / How shall I forget the broken shards/ and the scattered rice/ lying parched upon the earth? (see *MPT* 3/6).

Women poets too find their voice. Responding to a charge of being perceived as difficult and overtly feminist, Vatsala (1943 –) writes: 'Forgive me . . . / My poems –/ pieces of glass/ drenched in blood –/ pain you.// Tired from a day's work,/ reclining in an easy chair,/ what you need/ are lyrical poems/ that caress your heart' ('Glass pieces and jasmine flowers'). These are unambiguous, hard-hitting poems, challenging to write in a society that frowns upon such honesty.

In 'Do you understand', Urvashi (1956 –) writes: 'I am not particularly a soft-natured woman/ nor am I as naïve as I once was. / Our current state of affairs/ gives me no signs for hope. / It is certain / . . . / we must be apart. / Then, / why should I stay within this house/

any longer? / Well, / Do you understand what I write to you?' Salma
(1968 –) talks unashamedly of the female body, post childbirth: 'You
are much repelled/ you say, / by a thickened body/ and a belly criss-
crossed with birthmarks . . .' These poems break free of tradition with
immediacy and urgency, in the spoken voice, addressing the reader
directly.

Interior Decoration is an ambitious anthology; it introduces us to fifty-
four women poets from ten Indian languages. Apart from Kamala Das
and Suganthi Subramanian (both died in 2009), the remaining living
poets in *Interior Decoration* write not only about issues that define
them, but collectively explore 'the nature of censorship that women
face' – be it by the state, the market, community leaders, society at
large, families, even themselves.

A gallery image of Indian women emerges through several sharp
vignettes: 'A woman is a thing apart. / She is bracketed off, a/ Comma,
semi colon at most/ A lower case letter, lost// In the literate circus./
. . . , but when she speaks/ Her poems bite, ferocious' ('Margins, Ma(i)
nstream' by Rukmini Bhaiya Nair, English). Seeking a 'new language/
In which to hold her own', she is branded a witch: 'One who writes
poetry in the middle of the night/ with her hair undone is a witch'
('The Witch' by Mandakranta Sen, Bengali). Women here write
in blood: 'Buried deep/ in the lines of writers,/ I didn't learn/ from
where/ those quills/ shed drops of blood' ('Ignorance' by Lalitha Lenin,
Malayalam).

A new way of relating is insisted upon in a world where women
are read 'casually/ like one reads the torn pages/ of a child's notebook/
before it is made into paper-cones'. The poet, Anamika, says: 'read
us carefully/ one word at a time/...// Look at us with yearning/ as,
shivering, you would look at a fire out of reach. // Listen to us/ as you
would the soundless void/ and try to understand, slowly/ a language
newly learned.' ('Women' by Anamika, Hindi). Such messages are
aimed at men and society at large.

Challapalli Swaroopa Rani (Telugu) asks: 'When has my life been
truly mine?/ In the home male arrogance/ Sets my cheek stinging/
While on the street caste arrogance/ Splits the other cheek open'
('Wild Flower'). Needless to mention, there is a lot of protest. 'Revolt
flows constantly in my veins/ I am an eternally bleeding wound,' writes
Saroop Dhruv (Gujrati) in 'I'; she also asserts: 'Here I am, as strong as

a foundation/ a root, a base; like grammar.' There is a need to reinvent oneself through a new language.

Shahjahana (Telugu) despairs of 'how many dreams are slaughtered/ behind each veil/ how many desires/ how many hopes/ lie smashed behind dark veils'. ('Lift that Veil') In 'Dignity' Bilqees Zefirul Hasan (Urdu) writes: 'Self-respect *is something*; but how should Dhaniya make/ Bibi Sahab understand this?' Here are two women, Bibi Sahab is the lady of the house, Dhaniya is her servant; they share a common fate – drunken, miserly husbands. Dhaniya could not live with her man; Bibi stays on for 'the dignity she attains by living with her husband'. Women do not really have choices. 'Unable to dissolve the poverty line ever/ I decided to sell my breasts. / Upon losing all other organs in an auction/ I went to shop after shop...' (Kutti Ravathi (Tamil), 'Not for sale'). These are devastating indictments of Indian society.

There is hope too. It is reassuring to read Rose Mary (Malayalam): 'Like one emperor to another,/ like one friend to another,/ come to me/ as an equal./ .../ like the question/ seeking its answer/ may your steps be/ as light/ and as carefree...' Here are poems that speak for themselves, honestly and confidently; they speak of the pain and pleasure of being a woman for 'that's when the poem writes itself'. ('Epitaph' by Menka Shivdasani, English).

Shanta Acharya

Further Reviews

Martinus Nijhoff
Awater, translated by David Colmer,
James S. Holmes, Daan Van Der Vat from Dutch,
edited by Thomas Mohlmann
Anvil Press Poetry
112pp, paperback, ISBN 9780856464072

Ilija Jovanović
News from the Other World
Poems in Romani, translated by Melitta Depner
Francis Boutle Publishers
153pp, paperback, ISBN 9781903427545

Minority not Minorities: A Window on Italian Cultures Volume 1
Poets from Sardinia, edited by Michele Pinna,
translated by Giuseppe Serpillo, Andrea Bianchi,
Silvana Siviero, Robert Minhinnick
Cinnamon Press
110pp, paperback, ISBN 9781907090394

Joan Margarit
New Letters to a Young Poet, translated by Christopher Maurer
Swan Isle Press
120pp, hardback, ISBN 9780974888194 $24.00

Joan Margarit
Strangely Happy, translated by Anna Crowe
Bloodaxe Books,
160pp, paperback, ISBN 9781852248932 £9.95

For the first time Anvil Poetry Press have brought together Martinus
Nijhoff's long poem *Awater* with the first English translation by Daan
van der Vat (1949) and the two subsequent translations by James S
Holmes (1961) and David Colmer (2010).

Readers can now be acquainted with the mysterious *Awater* in the original Dutch and through the later resurrections. Billed as the most important Dutch poem of the 20th century, translations of the poem were originally published in periodicals – James S Holmes' in *MPT* 27-8, in 1976.

Accompanying the poem are notes, letters, essays, including Nijhoff's excellent 'Poetry in a period of Crisis', which discusses the genesis of the name 'Awater'. Who is Awater? According to Nijhoff 'Awater was to be an arbitrary individual with whom I had no personal ties. Awater had to be the name for one person but he was to remain abstraction and multitude.'

The poem is inescapably haunting. Daan van der Vat found himself in 'a nightmare state' as the poem demands a concentration that creates a penetrating intimacy: 'I felt an aversion to the very thought of giving up all my distance to it by setting to work on a translation.' Daan van der Vat was assisted in his translation, through a series of conversations and letters with Nijhoff; the translation met with his approval and owes its existence to Daan van der Vat's insistence on making it available to readers of English. The later translations offer a valuable comparison and a sense of how English language and syntax have evolved. Awater's after-life has been handled sensitively by James S Holmes, whilst David Colmer has taken a more academic approach. It is Daan van der Vat's original translation that sits closely to the spirit of the poem, though it may be lacking in poetic ambition. Collectively the translations allow Awater's continuing presence to pass through language and time.

'Lesser used languages of Europe' is the title of the series of books from Francis Boutle Publishers whose forthcoming anthologies include Scottish Gaelic, Esperanto and Cornish. Recent titles include anthologies of Manx and Breton literature. The series focuses on Europe's minority languages and dialects, with valuable introductions that allow for greater access to the traditions and social history of each language.

The Gurbet dialect of Romani is celebrated in *News from the other World*, a single collection by the Roma poet Ilija Jovanović, with translations by Melitta Depner. Included is a moving memoir of Jovanović's childhood, detailing the Romanies' spring migration to more fertile villages, including the notorious village Jarak and the half-understood stories of Jarak as a site for a Nazi concentration camp. A necessary addition to the poems is an essay on the Roma people and the origins of the Romani language: 'the oldest living example of the Indo-European languages'. The essay prefaces the poems, which are delicate and heartfelt in their small gestures against a backdrop of hunger, wandering and discrimination:

Looking for peace

Let us go there
where hearts
are full of love,
and where people willingly share
their bread with us.

Let us go
to that far place,
where people love one another
and where they hug and kiss.

Let us go
to that hidden place,
where humans
look for and find themselves
in their fellow human beings.

Cinnamon Press and a team of highly skilled editors and translators with the Istituto Bellieni have brought out the first of a series of anthologies demonstrating the vitality of Sardinian Poetry. A lively translator's introduction describes segmented processes of working through Sardinian to Italian to English. The anthology features the work of ten prize-winning bilingual Italian poets: Alcioni, Canu, Cocco, Cherchi, Delogu, Mura Ena, Piras, Porcheddu, Rubattu and Serra.

The editor Michele Pinna describes how each of authors represents the different territorial areas, 'including an area reserved to a linguistic minority, that of the minority of Alghero (North Sardinia) through the poems of Antonio Canu'. Both Raffaele Piras and Anna Cristina Serra also write in the Campidanese variety of Sardinian. Although recognised as a language in its own right, Sardinian is still classified in some Libraries under *Linguistica italiana* (Italian linguistics), *Dialetti italiani* (Italian dialects). This is not a setback for a language that operates outside of formal settings and retains its poetic freedom 'to open, with its creative force, new horizons and new existential possibilities; all this through a language that is not the official one because the States, for well-known political reasons, have relegated all natural language to private and informal spheres in Europe'.

Despite the social and political constraints the translations and original poems are impressive. Franco Cocco's poems are particularly luminous:

> I have lost the North Star
> and
>   Orion
> and
>   the Pleiades
> and
>   the Milky Way
> and to add to my misery even
> this   little morsel
> of intelligence star of mine
> sending sudden flashes
> when vesper starts to dawn . . .
>
> but I am left with the moon
> the skies daily stranger
> lanterns of visions
> lit to dissipate the abyss of death . . .

In *New Letters to a Young Poet* Joan Margarit reveals how he wished he hadn't published his first book, which was written in Spanish: 'I had written it in 1960–61 at the age of 22 or 23, when I was totally devoted to the poetry of Neruda, and I hadn't learned that it isn't enough to immerse yourself in the world of masters: you must also leave it.'

Thankfully, Margarit hasn't quite left Rilke's *Letters to a Young Poet* behind but has absorbed Rilke's advice during his poetic career and has used that valuable companionship to enrich his own creative process. Margarit's candour and ability to justify his own poetics moves the book beyond the genres of poetics and literary critism. Almost approaching memoir, his defence of poetry has a concerned and fatherly tone: 'Poetry isn't the antechamber of solitude, it *is* solitude . . . The young poet should think that his apprenticeship to poetry is, at the the same time, an apprenticeship to solitude.' Marguerite Duras says much the same in 'Writing':

> The solitude of writing is a solitude without which writing could not be produced, or would crumble, drained bloodless by the search for something else to write. When it loses its blood, its authorstops recognising it.

Rilke, without doubt, has the last word on the subject: 'I know no advice for you save this: to go into yourself and test the deeps in which your life takes rise; at its source you will find the answer to the question whether you *must* create.'

After a silence of ten years – perhaps pondering Rilke's words – Joan Margarit embraced his Catalonian heritage: 'It wasn't until 1975, when I was 37 and Joaquim Marco published 'Crónica', in *Ocnos*, his mythical collection, that I first recognized a voice finally my own.'

Strangely Happy is consistently entrancing, the poems are unique experiences, suggesting the reader creates, witnesses and feels all the complexities and simplicities, within the poems. These are indeed strangely happy poems that confront without lingering in sentimentality and find resolution through bare-hearted honesty and a gentleness of tone that has been skilfully retained in the translations. (See *MPT* 3/6 for poems of Joan Margarit translated by Anna Crowe.)

Saradha Soobrayen

Notes on Contributors

Shanta Acharya was born in Orissa, India; she completed a doctoral thesis at Oxford and was a Visiting Scholar at Harvard. Her study, *The Influence of Indian Thought on Ralph Waldo Emerson*, was published in 2001. Her latest poetry collection is *Dreams That Spell The Light* (Arc Publications, 2010). Her poems have appeared widely in the UK, USA, and India. *www.shantaacharya.com*

Peter Kayode Adegbie is a Christian missionary, poet, filmmaker and cultural entrepreneur. He is president of Maximum Impact Leadership Academy and creator of a community project, 'Changing Perspectives', an oral history web portal and multimedia educational archival resource. He serves on the boards of several UK charities.

Alev Adil's first collection of poetry *Venus Infers* was published in 2004. She is Head of the Department of Communication and Creative Arts at the University of Greenwich.

Shon Arieh-Lerer's poems, translations, and reviews have appeared in magazines such as *Circumference*, *Beloit Poetry Journal*, *Chronogram*, and *World Literature Today*. His poem 'Chickasaw Silence' received a 2008 Our American Indian Heritage Award citation. He lives in Brooklyn, New York.

Gerry Byrne was born and grew up in Dublin. In 1986 he moved to England and trained first as a psychiatric nurse and then as a psychoanalytic child psychotherapist and works in Oxford. He is co-founder of Children in Troubled Worlds and with two colleagues runs an annual conference that invites speakers from the fields of art, literature, and psychoanalysis.

James Byrne was born near London in 1977. His second collection, *Blood/Sugar*, was published by Arc in November 2009. He is presently co-editing *Bones Will Crow: 16 Contemporary Burmese Poets*, due from Arc in 2012. He edits *The Wolf* poetry magazine and lives in Cambridge.

Nancy Campbell was writer-in-residence at Upernavik Museum, Greenland, during winter 2010, an undertaking in part funded by Arts Council England. Her most recent publication is the artist's book *How to say 'I love you' in Greenlandic: an Arctic alphabet*, and she is completing a collection of poems on traditional hunting practices in the High Arctic.

Alex Cigale's poems have appeared in *Colorado, Green Mountains, North American* and *St. Petersburg* reviews. His translations from the Russian are in *Crossing Centuries: the New Generation in Russian Poetry, Modern Poetry in Translation,* and *PEN America 12 Correspondences* issue. He was born in Chernovtsy, Ukraine and lives in New York City.

Murray Citron spoke Yiddish as a child. He came recently on the poetry of Itzik Manger and is recovering his Yiddish to read the poems.

Ken Cockburn has published two books of poems, *Souvenirs and Homelands* (1998) and *On the flyleaf* (2007), and a collection of translations, *Feathers & Lime* (2007). In 2010, with Alec Finlay, he received a Creative Scotland Vital Spark award for *The Road North*, a 'translation' of Basho to contemporary Scotland (www.theroadnorth. co.uk)

Among **Peter Constantine's** recent translations are Sophocles' *Three Theban Plays* and *The Essential Writings of Machiavelli*. He is a 2010 Guggenheim Fellow, and was awarded the PEN Translation Prize for *Six Early Stories by Thomas Mann*, and the National Translation Award for *The Undiscovered Chekhov*.

Peter V. Czipott holds a Ph. D. in physics and provides consultation services in applied physics and renewable energy. As a literary translator with John M. Ridland, he has published translations of poems by György Faludy, Miklós Radnóti, Bálint Balassi, and Sándor Márai in journals in the U.S., U.K., and Australia.

Iain Galbraith's recent publications include the poetry anthology *Beredter Norden. Schottische Gedichte seit 1900* (Edition Rugerup, 2011) and translated volumes by John Burnside (*Versuch über das Licht*, Carl Hanser Verlag, 2011) and W. G. Sebald *Across the Land and the Water. Selected Poems 1964–2001* (Hamish Hamilton, 2011).

Delphine Grass has published poems in both French and English poetry magazines such as *A Verse*, *Magma* and *The Black Herald*. She is finishing a Ph.D. on the French writer Michel Houellebecq at UCL and has translated his poetry collection *Le Sens du combat* (The Art of Struggle) with Timothy Mathews.

Philip Gross's *The Water Table* (Bloodaxe) won the T.S.Eliot Prize 2009. *I Spy Pinhole Eye* (Cinnamon) won Wales Book of The Year 2010 and *Off Road To Everywhere* (Salt) the CLPE award for children's poetry 2011.

Nilanjan Hajra is a poet and journalist based in Kolkata, India.

David Hart was long since a university chaplain in Birmingham, then a theatre critic, after that an arts administrator and for fifteen years or so now works as a poet. He has held hospital, cathedral and festival residencies. His books include *Running Out* (Five Seasons Press, 2006).

Stuart Henson's most recent collection is *A Place Apart* (Shoestring Press). His new book *The Odin Stone* is due from Shoestring in 2011.

Norbert Hirschhorn is a public health physician, commended by President Bill Clinton as an 'American Health Hero'. He lives in London and Beirut. He has published two collections: *A Cracked River* (Slow Dancer Press, London, 1999), and *Mourning in the Presence of a Corpse* (Dar al-Jadeed, Beirut, 2008). www.bertzpoet.com.

Henry Israeli is founder and President of Saturnalia Books and teaches in the English Department at Drexel University. His collections include *New Messiahs* and *Praying to the Black Cat*. He is editor and co-translator of two editions of Luljeta Lleshanaku published by New Directions in the US and a co-translator of her *Haywire: New & Selected Poems* (Bloodaxe Books, 2011).

Marina Della Putta Johnston is a Lecturer in Italian at the University of Pennsylvania. Although her primary focus is the relation between words and illustrations in Medieval and Renaissance texts, Pasolini's poetry is especially dear to her because it resounds with the musical language of her childhood in Friuli, Italy.

Ilmar Lehtpere has translated seven books by Kristiina Ehin, including Popescu Prize winner *The Drums of Silence* (Oleander 2007), PBS Recommended Translation *The Scent of Your Shadow* (Arc 2010) and, most recently, *The Final Going of Snow* (*MPT* Poets 2011). Three new Kristiina Ehin translations are in preparation.

Hubert Moore recently retired as a writing mentor of survivors of torture at the Medical Foundation. His seventh collection, *A garment of two greens*, is due from Shoestring Press early in 2012.

David Morley has won fourteen writing awards and a National Teaching Fellowship. *Enchantment* (Carcanet, 2010) was a Sunday Telegraph Book of the Year. *The Invisible Kings* (2007) was a PBS Recommendation. His creative writing podcasts are among the most popular literature downloads on iTunes worldwide. He is Professor of Writing at Warwick University. www.davidmorley.org.uk

Christopher Pilling's translation of Tristan Corbière's *Les Amours Jaunes* (*These Jaundiced Loves*) was published by Peterloo Poets in 1995 (only available now from chrispilling@onetel.com). He is also a translator of Catullus, Max Jacob, Lucien Becker and Maurice Carême. His own poems are gathered in *Coming Ready or Not* (Bookcase, Carlisle 2009).

Shpresa Qatipi is a professor of English at Tirana University. In addition to many poems by Luljeta Lleshanaku, she has translated and published short stories, essays, and articles for the Eurolindja Publishing House in Albani and the Soros Foundation.

John M. Ridland translated Sándor Petöfi's *János Vitéz* (*John the Valiant*) in 1999. Besides translations with Peter Czipott, he has published his own poems in a dozen books and chapbooks and in journals from *Poetry* and the *Hudson Review* to *Quadrant* (Australia). His translation of *Sir Gawain and the Green Knight* is being published in instalments in Michoacán, Mexico.

Michael Rosen was born in 1946 and brought up in north-west London. He studied English at Wadham College, Oxford, did an MA and a Ph.D in children's literature, and 2007–2009 was Children's Laureate. He has always spent a good deal of time in France and regularly works at the Institut Français in London.

David Shook studied poetry and translation at Oxford. He lives in Los Angeles, where he edits *Molossus* and publishes Phoneme Books. Recent translations include a chapbook of Víctor Terán's poetry, Oswald de Andrade's *Cannibal Manifesto*, and Mario Bellatin's *Shiki Nagaoka: A Nose for Fiction*. Many of his recent translations are available on his website, at <http://davidshook.net>.

Taije Silverman's debut book of poetry, *Houses Are Fields*, was published in 2009. New work is forthcoming in *Agni, The Harvard Review,* and elsewhere. She is the 2010-2011 W.K. Rose Fellow and was a 2011 Fulbright Fellow in Italian poetry at the University of Bologna.

Cameron Hawke Smith was born in Cambridge in 1945 and has degrees in Classics and Archaeology. His poetry, translations and reviews have appeared in *PN Review, MPT, Acumen, Fourteen* and elsewhere. He has recently begun learning Gaelic from native speakers whilst undertaking an archaeological survey in the Western islands.

Saradha Soobrayen is a freelance poetry and reviews editor and works as mentor and coach providing professional development for emerging and established writers and artists. Her poetry appears in the *Red Anthology 2009, The Forward Anthology 2008*, and *Oxford Poets Anthology 2007*. She received an Eric Gregory Award in 2004.

Fiona Sze-Lorrain writes and translates in English, French and Chinese. Her recent work includes translation of Auxeméry's *Mingus, méditations* (Estepa Editions, 2011), prose translations of Hai Zi (Tupelo Press, forthcoming) and *Water the Moon* (Marick Press, 2010), an Honorable Mention for the 2011 Eric Hoffer Book Award. An editor at *Cerise Press*, she is also a *zheng* concertist.

ko ko thett is 'a poet by choice and Burmese by chance'. He is also an activist and analyst and has lectured, written, and commented extensively on Burma since the late 1990s. Since January 2011 ko ko thett has co-edited *Bones Will Crow: an anthology of Contemporary Burmese Poetry*, contributing over 90 translations.

Ned Thomas is the founder and Honorary President of the Mercator Institute at Aberystwyth University in Wales. His autobiographical memoir *Bydoedd* (Worlds) which is structured around the different linguistic worlds he has inhabited — has just been adjudged Welsh-language Book of the Year.

Rimas Uzgiris' poetry and translations have been widely published in the USA. He received his MFA in creative writing from Rutgers-Newark University. He also holds a Ph.D. in philosophy from the University of Wisconsin-Madison. His philosophical monograph, *Desire, Meaning, and Virtue: The Socratic Account of Poetry*, was published in 2009.

Teleri Williams spent her childhood in Libya and Turkey, and returned home to Wales via England before settling in the Languedoc in southern France. Her poems, articles and translations have appeared in *Planet, Poetry Wales* and *New Welsh Review*. Her sequence of poems *In Sight of the Sea* was published in 2007.

Karen McCarthy Woolf was born in London to English and Jamaican parents. Her pamphlet *The Worshipful Company of Pomegranate Slicers* was a *New Statesmen* book of the year and a PBS recommendation. She appears in *Ten New Poets: Spread the Word* (Bloodaxe, 2010). She is interested in process and form, which she explores on her blog www.opennotebooks.co.uk.

Elżbieta Wójcik-Leese regularly publishes translations of contemporary Polish poetry into English. She also translates Polish children's books and English-language poetry. As a translator and writer, she has been involved in the Metropoetica project — 'Poetry and Urban Space: Women writing cities' (www.metropoetica.org). The London Underground featured her translations in summer 2011.

Katerina and Elena Zhuravleva are sisters. Katerina is an artist and translator, Elena is a sociologist. Despite the differences in their professional choices they are both interested in English. Their acquaintance with Juri Vella gave them the opportunity to embark on the translation of fiction, and in 2011 their translation of *The Threads of Kinship* was published.

MPT Subscription Form

Name	Address
Phone	Postcode
E-mail	Country

I would like to subscribe to *Modern Poetry in Translation* (please tick relevant box):

Subscription Rates (including postage by surface mail)

	UK	Overseas
❏ One year subscription (2 issues)	£19.90	£25 / US$ 42
❏ Two year subscription (4 issues) with discount	£36	£46 / US$ 77

Student Discount*

❏ One year subscription (2 issues)	£16	£21 / US$ 35
❏ Two year subscription (4 issues)	£28	£38 / US$ 63

Please indicate which year you expect to complete your studies 20 . . .

Standing Order Discount (only available to UK subscribers)
❏ Annual subscription (2 issues)   £18
❏ Student rate for annual subscription (2 issues)*   £14

Payment Method (please tick appropriate box)

❏ **Cheque:** please make cheques payable to: *Modern Poetry in Translation.* Sterling, US Dollar and Euro cheques accepted.

❏ **Standing Order:** please complete the standing order request below, indicating the date you would like your first payment to be taken. This should be at least one month after you return this form. We will set this up directly with your bank. Subsequent annual payments will be taken on the same date each year. For UK only.

Bank Name Branch Address Post Code Sort Code Account Number	Account Name ❏ Please notify my bank Please take my first payment on ..../......./......... and future payments on the same date each year. Signature: Date........./........./............

Bank Use Only: In favour of Modern Poetry in Translation, Lloyds TSB, 1 High St, Carfax, Oxford, OX1 4AA, UK a/c 03115155 Sort-code 30-96-35

Please return this form to: The Administrator, Modern Poetry in Translation, The Queen's College, Oxford, OX1 4AW   administrator@mptmagazine/www.mptmagazine.com